Praise for *Make a Difference*

———◆••◆———

God admonishes older women to give good counsel and train younger women. *Make a Difference* tells of the legacy Joy is leaving through her mentoring relationship with Lindsey. Join them in this exciting journey of love and friendship!

—Joyce Meyer, best-selling author and Bible teacher

———◆••◆———

With the so-called revolutions in sexuality and gender sensitivities, too many women have lost sight of the beauty and the power of being a real woman. This book will help them regain some of that lost respect for femininity.

—Dr. Laura Schlessinger, radio host, author of *The Proper Care and Feeding of Husbands Handbook*

———◆••◆———

Our church with a heart began by having a mother with a heart. Joy and Lindsey share their meaningful lives through a deeply fulfilling friendship with Jesus and show that one plus one equals ten thousand!

—Tommy Barnett, Phoenix First Assembly

———◆••◆———

Is it ever OK for a Christian to be envious? I only had to read the first few pages of *Make a Difference* to know that I want a relationship like the one Joy Barnett and Lindsey Clifford have! May God continue to bless them, and may He use their book to stir the hearts of women to reach out to one another—even across generations.

—Michele Buckingham, writer and editor of more than 40 Christian books

———◆••◆———

Let's face it. Women are experts in shaaaarrrrring. Imagine the difference in your life and the ones you love as you read *Make a Difference*. You'll enjoy this practical book. Remember that God always uses people to change others' lives.

—Dr. Kevin Leman, psychologist, author of *The Birth Order Book*

A delightful example of the older woman teaching the younger woman, Joy and Lindsey's account will grip your heart. Filled with fascinating stories and practical help, this book illustrates the joy of living Jesus out in mentoring relationships. A timely read in a culture where women seeking resolutions to difficult issues through their relationship discovered the answers in Him.

—Sandee Fuller, Area Director, Community Bible Study

This book has such a precious lesson for us all throughout the storyline. I certainly have found mentoring relationships to be extremely important in my own life, in every area. I recommend this book to anyone seeking to enrich their lives through Godly relationships and growth.

—Betty J. Mohlenbrock, M. Ed., founder of Family Literacy Foundation

At its very heart, this is a book about love—God's beautiful, overwhelming, and all-encompassing love for us in Jesus Christ—and how we truly can experience that love in the blessings of our relationships with others. It is not about us, it's about Him pouring His love into and through us in the lives of those special ones He places in our path as we walk ever closer to Him. The greatest of these is love . . . love never fails.

—Bonnie Botsford, Horizon Christian Fellowship

We all need someone to talk to—someone who will listen to us, encourage us, and love us unconditionally. That's the kind of relationship Joy Barnett and Lindsey Clifford have developed over the years, and I'm happy for them. All of us can learn from their example.

—Jackie Buckingham, widow of author Jamie Buckingham, Director
of Hebron Ministries

The Dream Center's Mission of meeting tangible and spiritual needs is reaping a harvest of fruit from the seeds planted many years ago by my grandmother, who taught me God's natural laws lead us to God's spiritual principles. We have to feed the hungry first before teaching them the Gospel. You will learn her secrets to a happy loving life now in *Make a Difference*.

—Matthew Barnett, Dream Center Los Angeles

For a practical mentoring "how-to," *Make a Difference* is a must read. How a woman can expect to grow to her fullest God-given potential is beyond me without the nudging, tough love and unconditional support that come from a focused and committed Christian mentor. Using the example born out of their own precious relationship, Lindsey and Joy show us how it's done.

—Sylvia Lange, singer, Crimson Bridge Ministries

Make a Difference breaks new ground in reconciling significant relationships in a practical and stimulating way that gives the reader the confidence to dare to do the difficult in connecting and succeed.

—Laurie Beth Jones, author of *Jesus – CEO; The Path;* and *Jesus,
Life Coach*

Make a Difference provides excellent and practical principles for Christians to clearly understand Christ's calling and purpose in their lives.

—Bill and Vonette Bright, Campus Crusade for Christ,
blessed before his death

Make a Difference

Mentoring

Woman

to

Woman

Lindsey Clifford

and

Joy Barnett

www.makeadifferencementoring.com

This book is

dedicated to those

who have sought for the meaning

of the pieces

of their lives.

Contents

Acknowledgments

To. . . .

Courtney, Gabrielle, James, and Hannah,
for giving me permission to grow up with you
and teaching me tolerance and love
in ways no one else could.
You are each unique and appreciated
for who you are;
God meant you to be you!

Our families,
for your faith and belief in us.

Bruce Barbour,
our awesome agent who told me we had a book
and whose diplomatic encouragement brought it to life
while your holy spirituality kept it on course.

Richard Andrews and The Blanchard Team, Bob Botsford,
David Crawford, Al Ells, Steve Gottry, Mark Victor Hansen,
Kendell Lang, Kevin Leman, Sam Moore,
Ramona Richards, Troy Reichert, Karen Sparks,
Ted Squires, Elizabeth and John Williams,
Monique, Melissa and our many friends whose unprinted
names are forever imprinted in our hearts
with gratitude for your priceless contributions
of love, time, wisdom, and expertise
in making this book possible.

Michael,
for being my best advocate in letting me be who God
meant me to be. I appreciate you with all my heart.
This is your idea come to life!

Most of all,
Joy and Lindsey both give the glory to
our wonderful God, our precious Jesus, and our sweet Holy
Spirit for being with us in every area of our lives.
We love You!

"Mentoring helps give you a better life."
Hannah Clifford, age 7

Perspective

There is an urgent need in the heart of every person to make a difference. A journey of fulfillment begins with that need. Something inside you cries out for understanding, direction. Questions arise that find no answer, and the search goes on consciously or unconsciously.

We want to know our life counts. You may even feel God does not hear you. Then in one unexpected moment of time, you find yourself in the presence of someone you have just met and you want to know them—you need to know them. They feel familiar without prior knowledge.

My husband had just passed away from the church we pastored for 44 years. We planned on retiring together in Phoenix, but I now found myself on my own. I felt this deep, empty hole in my heart without my husband and without my identity. "Who am I, God? Where are You?" I prayed, feeling it was impossible to start over at age 63.

Getting involved at my son Tommy's church counseling and teaching the new Singles' Ministry was a good start even though it was an uncomfortable fit being single after 44 years of marriage. I knew the best way to find my identity was to get outside of myself and be a blessing to someone else.

Nothing happens by accident. God put Lindsey in my life as an answer to prayer although I did not know it at the time. When this beautiful young woman sat down next to me at a conference one evening, I unexpectedly felt better. I saw in her persona so much refinement and quality. From our conversation I saw her intellect, her potential in Jesus Christ, and I wanted to be a part of her life.

And then a wonderful thing happened. She too felt a connection, and we knew there was a fit. We began to move in God's planning, not even knowing exactly what it was. That is part of the process. We don't have to understand the process. If we understood, then the process would be lost and we wouldn't accomplish what God intended. Being compelled by God does more to keep us in His will than understanding His process would.

In the midst of my great loss, God was defining my identity to a greater degree. It is through heartache and unanticipated changes that you can find yourself by giving to others. Being in my 60s was not an excuse to stop being pliable; it was a reason to give more at a deeper level.

When Lindsey and I met, I wasn't thinking, "What's in this for me," rather, "What's in this for God?" I still wanted to be a blessing in the midst of my pain and loss. We never know what we're doing for the other person.

I was not always ready to give, but with Lindsey I was able to give because God had groomed me. We had no idea—we did not plan our friendship. Over the years, we poured into one another's lives the things that we needed because of God's love in each of us.

Lindsey and I needed each other. What is extremely significant is that Lindsey and I lived close by each other for only a year after we met. Occasionally, we would visit each other over the years, but the rest of our relationship was maintained over the telephone. And we don't talk. We communicate. God helped us walk together, enjoy each other, expand, and grow. There is almost an untouchable quality of mentoring that happens at such a deep level that you have to experience it in order to grasp it.

Lindsey and I had a comfortable fit we knew was from God. We held on to it and moved on it because we were being obedient to God's calling in us. As time went on in our lives, we communicated, shared, and blessed one another.

My need to bless people was fulfilled because I knew she was being blessed. She was being blessed because she could trust me. Everybody needs a trusted friend—someone you can talk to.

Through these things, our hearts were bonded together stronger than we even knew. It was God's answer to our unconscious prayers. God knows our hearts so well.

Our relationship brought a certain kind of tolerance for whatever we had to go through because there was one person on earth who truly understood. I believe the basis for a wonderful mentoring situation is gentle and unexpected. Yet we are in the mentoring process where two people bless and minister to one another for the very needs that only they know.

We never worked at it. I think that's the most important thing about mentoring.

Mentoring is not counseling although it may be included. Counseling helps you to understand what you should do, but mentoring enables you to do it because your mentor is walking through it with you.

Mentoring embodies the solution. What was fulfilling with Lindsey was seeing her ability and propensity reach their full potential. She learned how not to let the circumstances of life dim her ability to believe in herself. She thinks I just helped her stay the course, but she helped me keep my identity.

As we grow from infancy to maturity, the body is constantly struggling to make necessary adjustments. So it is with our spiritual growth. God knows how to stretch each area so that we can grow. It may hurt a little. We may not understand because if we understood, the real value of the process would be lost. But when we trust anyway and reach and search, we find new treasures in living that finally reveal to us why those things had to happen in our lives.

As I get older, I see the cycle of life as children marry and leave. And the people I used to know are one-by-one dying and leaving. I have learned that the seasons of life bring different identities to us at times.

There was a time when I was known as Hershel's wife and my children's mom. As I reflect on who I have been, I realize I am still the same person. The circumstances changed, but I did not. I find my identity in Jesus Christ and by blessing the people He puts in my path. You don't have to go looking for it. My identity is the same, but my description changes according to the circumstances and my seasons of life. I've learned not to let the circumstances dictate my identity. New generations come along to define us. When you get stuck in the past, you can't reach the present generation.

Because of this truth, Lindsey and I stand shoulder to shoulder bridging the generation gap. God initiated this plan, and the Holy Spirit enabled this plan to work. God's mentoring enables us to combine our strengths together. Mentoring reaches a place where it's not just to our needs; it goes far beyond that. Needs become strengths and are united. Strength together can put ten thousand to flight.

God mentoring us brought us to a level where instead of one plus one equals two, the multiplicative function took over. If one can put a thousand, two can put ten thousand to flight. This principle causes ministry growth. It's not just pounding people over the head! You can be right, use the right thing, and still destroy. Negative counseling without enabling and gentle mentoring will never teach the lesson you need to learn.

God planned it all. Jesus initiated it and made it possible. The Holy Spirit is here to lead us and to point us to Jesus. The Holy Spirit is our Mentor who walks with us to teach us, to comfort us, and to guide us into all truth. He is our Holy Mentor. God our Father, Jesus our Brother, the Holy Spirit our Mentor.

I want you to be blessed, enriched, and amazed as you read about relationships and people made great by God. You are about to encounter revealing revolutionary principles of living that will make a difference, help you the rest of your life, and propel you into deeper spiritual fulfillment!

Joy Barnett

"And I will ask the Father, and He will give you another Comforter (Counselor, Helper, Intercessor, Advocate, Strengthener, and Standby), that He may remain with you forever—The Spirit of Truth, Whom the world cannot receive (welcome, take to its heart), because it does not see Him or know and recognize Him . . . for He lives with you [constantly] and will be in you . . .
. . . the Comforter (Counselor, Helper, Intercessor, Advocate, Strengthener, Standby), the Holy Spirit, Whom the Father will send in My name [in My place, to represent Me and act on My behalf], Who will teach you all things. And He will cause you to recall (will remind you of, bring to your remembrance) everything I have told you."

John 14:16,17,26

"The Spirit of the Lord [is] upon Me, because He has anointed Me [the Anointed One, the Messiah] to preach the good news (the Gospel) to the poor;

*He has sent Me to announce release to the captives and recovery
of sight to the blind,
to send forth as delivered those who are oppressed [who are
downtrodden, bruised,
crushed, and broken down by calamity]."*

Luke 4:18

CHAPTER ONE
God Meant Us to Be

The lot is cast into the lap, but the decision is wholly of the Lord [even the events that seem accidental are really ordered by Him].

Proverbs 16:33

He has made everything beautiful in its time. He also has planted eternity in men's hearts and minds [a divinely implanted sense of a purpose working through the ages which nothing under the sun but God alone can satisfy], yet so that men cannot find out what God has done from the beginning to the end.

Ecclesiastes 3:11

"The glory of friendship is not the outstretched hand, nor the kindly smile, nor the joy of companionship; it is the spiritual inspiration that comes to one when he discovers that someone else believes in him and is willing to trust him with his friendship."

Ralph Waldo Emerson

We were meant to meet. I was young, feisty, full of life and full of myself, with most of my life still in front of me, yet to be lived. Joy Barnett was an elegant and regal woman, full of life and less of herself, with a lot of her life already lived, tamed, and molded by life's experiences and the wisdom that they brought and she employed.

When we met, she had already been a pastor's wife of 44 years and the mother of Tommy Barnett, the Pastor of Phoenix First Assembly, one of the largest churches in the U.S. He was my pastor, so I thought Joy had to be pretty outstanding, but that thought was only the tip of the iceberg. I did not know the future height of our relationship, like reaching the summit of Mt. Everest.

It was in the front row of a conference one evening that I happened to sit next to Joy. We became instant friends. God had planned this for a long time.

Like fresh produce ripe for eating, Joy passed the fruits of her mentoring on to me. This delicious fruit has been laden with vitamins and essential elements that have enriched me and helped make me strong and healthy.

In fact, I've picked, savored, eaten, and relished the fruit from Joy's vine for so many years that my own vine now produces fruit to be consumed by those in my life needing His nourishment. Sometimes we have a sense in our spirit that God has brought a particular person into our life and so it was with Joy.

According to Joy, "The seemingly accidental things are not accidental at all." The decision for us to sit together at that meeting was not an accident. God planned that wisely and carefully. The fact that we fit in personality and closeness was God's plan. He has put in you and me all the qualities we need to strengthen, bless, and help each other. "When we talked together for the first time, it was just right because it was God's plan from the beginning. He had worked carefully to put every piece in place."

We both saw the significance of what was meant to be. Just as God meant for us to have a deeply connected friendship, so we believe you were meant to read the wisdom of these words, take the taste test for yourself, and be the better for it! My mom used to say, "The real friends you have in life you can count on the fingers of one hand." She was right. And Joy is one of five.

We enjoy our fresh vegetables, like style more than

fashion, and can finish each other's sentences. Both of us get our second wind at midnight. We can laugh at ourselves, and we love people. Neither one of us is the "roll over and play dead" sort, so dying to ourselves was not easy.

Joy's lived the life worth following, worth living and worth dying to me. "Dying to self" simply means letting go of my way and doing it God's way. The last time we shopped together, we both bought twin jean jackets—size small. By the end of the night, I was running after Joy trying to keep up with her. What makes this most amazing? Joy is 86 and I'm 47. We are nearly two generations apart, but we have such fun together. To meet Joy is like discovering the fountain of youth. She walks straight with a smooth gait, no gravel in her voice, her hair in the latest—not oldest—style. She still wears stilettos to dress up, yet greets you in sneakers and jeans when winding down.

Just like purpose, mentoring is a principle, not a goal. And it becomes a process that produces a lot of life-giving fruit. Joy's mentoring me was not an end in itself. It was simply the result of a natural and nurtured friendship. I now live with greater purpose each day because of the principles I have gained from Joy's relational mentoring. She has taught me to look to God as my Source and to abide in Jesus, not in her friendship.

"You know," Joy said, "I had to have some help. And I knew that help could not come from any other person. It had to come from God injecting into my spirit an understanding of the situation and the knowledge and wisdom of how to deal with it. I learned a long time ago that without the wisdom and understanding from God Himself, I would not be able to survive.

"God became my only Source for one other reason. Sometimes you cannot really talk things through with a 'friend.' They don't have any more wisdom than you do about the situation. They have no more understanding about it than you do. It's something that only you and God are facing, and unless He comes through with the answer and makes things deeply understood and fully accepted by you, you will not be able to conquer the situation."

I was a pregnant young bride when we first met, and over 20 years later, Joy is still my dearest friend and spiritual mentor. Like a parent lowering the tree branch so the child can pick fruit, so Joy hears from God and translates powerful spiritual principles into simple, practical terms that are reachable, understandable, edible, and usable.

Through mentoring, the baton is passed from an older, wiser, experienced source to a younger, immature, inexperienced recipient. A mentor guides you through the defining moments (crises and major crossroads) in your life. Defining moments are those times when you choose how you will respond to a situation. They direct your destiny. Mentoring helps you make sound choices that have positive consequences.

Whether by biological relationship, friendship, discipleship, or training, mentoring is the process of passing wisdom and experience. Mentoring translates the timeless wisdom of God and His ancient servants to present-day reality where it may be practically applied. *Yet when we are among the full-grown (spiritually mature Christians who are ripe in understanding), we do impart a [higher] wisdom (the knowledge of the divine plan previously hidden); but it is indeed not a wisdom of this present age or of this world nor of the leaders and rulers of this age, who are being brought to nothing and are doomed to pass away. But rather what we are setting forth is a wisdom of God once hidden [from the human understanding] and now revealed to us by God—[that wisdom] which God devised and decreed before the ages for our glorification [to lift us into the glory of His presence]* (1 Co 2:6-7). Just as Paul describes, Joy imparted God's wisdom to me through her understanding, ripened by her maturity.

The relationships between Moses and Joshua and between Elijah and Elisha exemplify how mentoring portrays destiny. In Exodus 17:9, where Joshua first appears, Moses asked Joshua to fight Amalek. Joshua did as Moses said and defeated Amalek, laying down a lifelong foundation of spiritual recognition and faith. Their level of trust and dependence upon each other continued to grow and deepen. Moses relied heavily upon Joshua's loyalty and competence, while Joshua trusted Moses' wisdom and connection to God. They were mutually dependent upon the other's obedience to God's will. I believe Joshua was drawn to God's calling on his life through Moses' mentoring.

Moses took his young aide in Exodus 33:11, renamed him Joshua (Nu 13:16), sent him to explore the promised land (Nu 13:16-17), then commissioned, encouraged, and strengthened him (De 3:28). It is important to note that Moses did not tell Joshua what to do. Joshua had to hear from God Himself.

Moses' final act as a mentor was to pass the leadership of the Hebrews on to Joshua.

And Moses said to the Lord, let the Lord, the God of the spirits of all flesh, set a man over the congregation Who shall go out and come in before them, leading them out and bringing them in, that the congregation of the Lord may not be as sheep which have no shepherd. The Lord said to Moses, Take Joshua son of Nun, a man in whom is the Spirit, and lay your hand upon him; and set him before Eleazar the priest and all the congregation and give him a charge in their sight. And put some of your honor and authority upon him, that all the congregation of the Israelites may obey him. And Moses did as the Lord commanded him. He took Joshua and set him before Eleazar the priest and all the congregation, and he laid his hands upon him and commissioned him, as the Lord commanded through Moses.

Numbers 27:15-20,22-23

What Joshua saw in Moses, he put into practice. Joshua learned to take the problem to God, vent his feelings, praise God, believe God, and most of all, love God. All the Israelites died in the wilderness because they took problems to each other, complained, and remained in misery until they perished in the desert. Moses didn't die in the wilderness because he took the problem straight to the heart of God and talked to God.

After Moses died, God directly commissioned, encouraged, and strengthened Joshua, and Joshua directly obeyed the voice of God.

After the death of Moses the servant of the Lord, the Lord said to Joshua son of Nun, Moses' minister, Moses My servant is dead. So now arise [take his place], go over this Jordan, you and all this people, into the land which I am giving to them, the Israelites. No man shall be able to stand before you all the days of your life. As I was with Moses, so I will be with you; I will not fail you or forsake you. Be strong (confident) and of good courage. Have not I commanded you? Be strong, vigorous, and very courageous. Be not afraid, neither be dismayed, for the Lord your God is with you wherever you go.

Joshua 1:1,2,5,6,9

Moses' and Joshua's relationship was all about God! A mentor is a conduit, not an end. God was the Beginning and the End for both Moses and Joshua. God is the Beginning and the End for you and me! *I am the Alpha and the Omega, the First and the Last (the Before all and the End of all)* (Re 22:13).

Examples of mentoring are in movies like *Star Wars* (Obi-Wan Kenobi to Luke Skywalker) and *The Lord of the Rings* (Gandalf to Frodo). Even in the true story of *Seabiscuit*, C.S. Howard and Tom Smith's love and training to Red Pollard produced victories on Seabiscuit. These movies make defining moments wiser, passing their wisdom to their student, and their students' understanding. A defining moment is an instant in time where you make choices in a current situation that will affect the rest of your life. You can see the recognition register on their faces when their futures teeter between good and evil, whether or not to take the baton, and the choices they will make.

How do you become the fortunate recipient of famed wisdom and insight? Is it chance or choice? Does divine direction determine destiny? Or is there something else? Why are some people so successful with seemingly so little talent while others with great gifts go nowhere?

Mentoring is a phenomenon where the past meets the future in the present. So part of the answers to these questions may be that I let Joy's hindsight, which is almost always 20/20, become my insight and foresight. When I was younger, I would "jump the gun" and often make impulsive decisions without thinking or praying about them. "Why should I have to pray?"

I'd wonder to myself, seeing the answer so clearly, or so I thought. Joy would "talk to God" about something as if He were sitting at the breakfast table with her. Sometimes it would seem a little crazy to me. Initially, I accepted this because I accepted Joy, but now I too "talk to God."

Joy has a spirit of peace I have always found attractive. Over the years, I have realized this spirit of peace is actually her abiding in Jesus, and Jesus always precludes everything in her life—from the way she thinks to how she acts. The more I abide in Jesus, the more I see and sense this same peace in my thoughts and actions.

The story of our friendship and how we met proves that mentoring works. As it worked in our friendship, it also works in relationships where wisdom and experience are passed on at work, in school, in athletics, or any other field of interest. The principle and process of mentoring will work for anyone, and everyone has a story to tell. What's yours?

Gail was in her late 20s when she was impacted by the wisdom and love of Nicole. Gail explained, "I had gone to work for a church that never had a woman on staff before. And as I was secretary to one of the pastors on staff, the church hired Nicole to be an associate pastor for women's ministry. Then I became secretary to both.

"I was quite enamored by her because our senior pastor who asked her to come on board spoke very highly of her. It was a great honor to work with someone so highly esteemed by my pastor, but I was curious about a woman who had a pastoral role because I had never associated with a woman pastor before.

"As we began working together, the first two things I saw about her character were her humility and grace. Nicole's position and presence was especially disconcerting to many of the men who objected to a woman having an equal position with them. But I saw her humility and her grace with every one of them.

"Nicole prepared Bible studies for the women in church, and I typed them, gleaning her wisdom and knowledge of God's Word and how she imparted this. It was common knowledge in the church that if you didn't find Gail at her secretary's desk, then she was in Nicole's office. I was so intrigued by this woman whom God obviously had anointed and was using in the church in a very powerful way."

Their level of trust and dependence upon each other continued to grow and deepen. Nicole relied heavily upon Gail's dependability and support while Gail trusted Nicole's wisdom and God-connection.

"I was growing just being her secretary. However, the day came when I resigned to be a full-time mom. She approached me one afternoon. 'Gail, please come into my office.' We sat down and Nicole thoughtfully began, 'Gail, I really believe the Lord has called you to teach. . . .'

"And my thoughts quickly responded, 'I don't have any type of education to be a teacher. I don't feel qualified! Besides, there are so many other older women who should be doing this. I'm only 29.' I heard my voice betray my thoughts, 'Oh Nicole, I've always known you heard from the Lord, but this is the first time I believe you may have made a mistake.'

"Nicole laughed. 'Gail, you go home and pray about it and see if the Lord would speak to you about this.' I agreed. With the onset of summer, a family vacation provided an opportune time to be alone with my thoughts.

"Sitting there, staring at the ocean horizon, I bowed my head, 'Lord, You know I have every doubt that I am not called to teach, but I believe Nicole heard from You, and if there should be evidence that You want me to teach, then please show me.' "

Gail could hardly believe what happened next. Her Bible fell open to the most confirming Word she ever experienced: *Say not, I am only a youth; for you shall go to all to whom I shall send you, and whatever I command you, you shall speak.* (Je 1:7). That defining moment changed her life forever. Gail knew her calling was secure.

Upon her return, she sat down with Nicole and confirmed, "Nicole, I do believe that the Lord has called me to teach, but I'm not confident that I am capable—the Lord will give me the words.

Nicole countered, "Well, Gail, why do you think the Lord would ask you to teach?"

Gail pondered, "The only experience I've had in sharing something I'm passionate about is a study on husband-wife relationships. And that particular study changed my life."

Nicole smiled. "That's the one last slot I have open that needs to be filled for the fall. Would you prepare to teach on marriage relationships?"

Gail's ministry was birthed all because one woman's mentoring gave her the wisdom, life, and encouragement she needed to learn to stand on her own. Gail was young, she knew it, and she was humble enough to admit it to herself and to God and let God do the rest.

Just as Nicole and Gail were meant to meet, so it was for Alexandra and Francesca. Alexandra grew up in an alcoholic family and met Jesus when she was 19. She was immediately drawn by His calling on her life. Thinking, "If I didn't know about this plan of salvation, how many other people don't know?" she began to knock on doors and share Jesus with everyone in her neighborhood. She wasn't aware that most church members didn't witness door-to-door.

Within six months, she led five women to the Lord. Every Thursday morning, she went to the cul-de-sac where they lived and studied the Bible with them. Alexandra didn't know what to teach them except what her pastor taught on Sunday. When he would teach, she took notes then taught her little congregation.

Alexandra's ministry was born. "I've always had a heart for women and wanted to see women be allowed to come into their destiny," she said. "I never was told that I had limitations on my life until I got into the church, and then I always felt a call to preach and my pastor would tell me that wasn't what women should do. And that disheartened me. As I've gotten older, I just spent my life raising up women . . . mentoring women. And I go to countries to minister to women, and my message is always to tell women that they have value and there's so much they can do. I went five times during the Bosnian war, and ministered to Muslim women and they readily accepted Jesus."

Alexandra has mentored many women, sharing her life in mission work around the world through her ministry. She trains and mentors American Christian women who in turn reach out to oppressed women around the world, including Muslim women who have been so receptive to Jesus.

Then Alexandra met Francesca. Their friendship marked a pivotal change in both of their lives which God would use to fulfill His purposes in them individually and together. On one of Alexandra's trips, Francesca went with her. They immediately felt a natural rapport with each other and worked well together in the mission field. Alexandra appreciated Francesca's help while Francesca valued Alexandra's wisdom and experience. She recalled, "The Lord spoke to me and said, 'She's been through healing, she's been through deliverance, but she has to be re-parented by someone in the ministry because there's such a high call on her life. She'll never walk in her rightful place until she sees that there are people of integrity in the ministry who will love her.' I knew that was a mandate the Lord gave me.

"So I became like a mother to Francesca. And I just loved her through a lot of things, letting her live with us and sharing my life with her. Since she was never allowed to speak up or be upset at anybody, I would allow her to be upset with me. And I would walk with her through it, through things. We worked through so many things. I think a lot of people won't let others vent.

"Unless allowed to share your feelings and really vent, I don't know how you're going to get over so much. Many people have so many things to get through. And another thing that I have seen with women is they never allow the person they're mentoring to walk beside them. The mentor walks over the student. And unless you've come to the place to where that person walks beside you and is your peer, you haven't finished your job."

Mentoring worked for Alexandra and Francesca because they let the principle of mentoring become a process, producing eternal results. They both understood they were meant to meet so Francesca could become all God meant her to be. In return, she has been a blessing to Alexandra, completing the call on Francesca's life.

We want to share our experience, strength, and hope through the power of our destined friendship. We've made major investments in each other's lives, and we have both reaped rich rewards.

"Most men lead lives of quiet desperation and go to the grave with the song still in them," said Henry David Thoreau. Joy showed me how to sing as she has sung her life. Now we sing on pitch together.

Joy has passed to me some practical fundamentals and secrets of living that are now successfully fulfilled in my life.

If any of you is deficient in wisdom, let him ask of the giving God [Who gives] to everyone liberally and ungrudgingly, without reproaching or faultfinding, and it will be given him. Every good gift and every perfect (free, large, full) gift is from above; it comes down from the Father of all [that gives] light, in [the shining of] Whom there can be no variation [rising or setting] or shadow cast by His turning [as in an eclipse]. But the wisdom from above is first of all pure (undefiled); then it is peace-loving, courteous (considerate, gentle). [It is willing to] yield to reason, full of compassion and good fruits; it is wholehearted and straightforward, impartial and unfeigned (free from doubts, wavering, and insincerity).

James 1:5,17; 3:17

This happened through our friendship and God's wisdom manifest in us both. Mentoring worked for us, and it will work for you.

"When I think about how we were meant to meet and I understand it was God's purpose," reflects Joy, "in my heart and in my imagination I begin to see a beautiful mosaic that God has made from our lives. In that beautiful mosaic, He chose all the special pieces that He had already designed, cut, and fashioned for that particular mosaic.

"In each one of them, He had touched a little point and the circumstance came it into view. In another place, He touched and put a decision in somebody's mind. He put a person at a special place, and so on. And all the pieces of the mosaic, the pieces of my life and your life, began to fall into picture-perfect place. God has a plan . . . His purpose was brought about because it was meant to be."

Learn how to identify and value relationships that have impacted your life. You were meant to meet them. Remember, it's not where you start that counts. It's where you end up.

Personal Process Assessment

Joy and I were meant to meet. God meant us to be in each other's lives to fulfill a common destiny for both of us. She was a gifted leader's wife. I was a leader's wife, but a diamond in the rough who needed a lot of chiseling. God put someone in my life He knew I would listen to and could trust. Joy felt my love for her, saw a lot of herself in me, and envisioned a bright future. Who are those people in your life God meant you to meet?

As you read, we want you to ask God to show you those relationships in your life that point you to Him. God gives us good relationships to fulfill His purposes and to glorify Him; they are not to be an end in themselves. And because Jesus loves you, those relationships will produce loving results. The hallmark of a Godly mentor is the willingness to give God the glory for it all. Who is pushing you closer to Jesus?

I am the True Vine, and My Father is the Vinedresser. Any branch in Me that does not bear fruit [that stops bearing] He cuts away (trims off, takes away); and He cleanses and repeatedly prunes every branch that continues to bear fruit, to make it bear more and richer and more excellent fruit. You are cleansed and pruned already, because of the word which I have given you [the teachings I have discussed with you]. Dwell in Me, and I will dwell in you. [Live in Me, and I will live in you.] Just as no branch can bear fruit of itself without abiding in (being vitally united to) the vine, neither can you bear fruit unless you abide in Me. I am the Vine; you are the branches. Whoever lives in Me and I in him bears much (abundant) fruit. However, apart from Me [cut off from vital union with Me] you can do nothing. If a person does not dwell in Me, he is thrown out like a [broken-off] branch, and withers; such branches are gathered up and thrown into the fire, and they are burned. If you live in Me [abide vitally united to Me] and My words remain in you and continue to live in your hearts, ask whatever you will, and it shall be done for you. When you bear (produce) much fruit, My Father is honored and glorified, and you show and prove yourselves to be true followers of Mine. I have loved you, [just] as the Father has loved Me; abide in My love [continue in His love with Me]. If you keep My commandments [if you continue to obey My instructions], you will abide in My love and live on in it, just as I have obeyed My Father's commandments and live on in His love. I have told you these things, that My joy and delight may be in you, and that your joy and gladness may be of full measure and complete and overflowing. This is My commandment: that you love one another [just] as I have loved you. No one has greater love [no one has shown stronger affection] than to lay down (give up) his own life for his friends. You are My friends if you keep on doing the things which I command you to do.

John 15:1-14

CHAPTER TWO
Defining Moments

*Who comforts (consoles and encourages) us in every trouble
(calamity and affliction), so that we may also be able to comfort
(console and encourage) those who are in any kind of trouble
or distress, with the comfort (consolation and encouragement)
with which we ourselves are comforted (consoled and
encouraged) by God.*

2 Corinthians 1:4

*. . . (lead a life) worthy of the [divine] calling to which you have
been called.*

Ephesians 4:1

*Absence diminishes commonplace passions and increases great
ones, as the wind extinguishes candles and kindles fire.*

La Rouchefoucaulde (1613-1680)

Defining moments reveal your purpose. They are those moments in time when your choices define you and show your worth. There is a reason for it all, and your life counts.

Right now, no matter where you are, no matter what you've done or been through, God has His Hand on every minute detail. And whether or not you realize it, He is using every bit of it for good in your life.

This means by the very nature of your circumstances and because of Who God is, the things that have cost you the most will probably bring you the greatest reward.

Meeting Joy was a defining moment. It was a moment when I unconsciously made the choice that I was going to be her friend. This moment would change my life forever. I wanted a relationship with this outstanding person. Perhaps it was Jesus' reflection in her life, although I didn't see it that way at the time; I was still too immature. Not until I developed my own hindsight did I comprehensively see Joy for who she was and Whom she represented and reflected.

It is easy to misidentify our feelings, especially when we deal with the symptom and not the root. She was confident, and I was cocky. I thought I was confident, but I really had a lot of insecurity inside. Her quiet confidence coupled with her sharp mind made her fun to be with.

Joy was my friend first and then my mentor. We were kindred spirits and never thought or considered the dimension of mentoring. It was the natural result of a deep and lasting relationship because we fulfilled each others' needs.

"Let me tell you what I needed," Joy shared with me. "I was so full of the things that God had helped me to understand. Not a lot of words that I wanted to say to you, but I just wanted to share with you . . . some kind of very special belonging to a real, wonderful person. I knew that you were wonderful. I felt in my spirit God had great potential for you, but you didn't know what it was.

"You were searching for it, and I needed to be there for you to help you stabilize your walk with God until that you reached out and touched something very wonderful. I didn't know what that was, but God knew. God didn't tell you as I don't always tell people all the things I understand about their futures. I don't want to say that I'm a clairvoyant. I don't mean that."

Joy had lived long enough to see and understand that certain attitudes and actions have predictable consequences. Part of understanding is keeping your wisdom to yourself, which she wisely did with me.

Joy continued, "Only God knows the future. I knew we were on the right track in our relationship, so I felt close to God when I saw you. That built me up spiritually, knowing that God is doing something, and I am a part of it."

Mentors help fill our basic needs for love, belonging, and maturity in certain areas of our lives. Mentors also help meet our deep need for spiritual fulfillment and understanding. Within the context of our relationship, Joy met my need for spiritual fulfillment and emotional maturity in the capacities of a mother and a leader's wife. I met her needs of being loved, wanted, and needed.

"I knew it was something bigger than us," said Joy, "but I didn't know what it was. By my being there and loving you, I don't know when it happened, but I always knew you loved me and that meant so much to me. I always felt it was for this binding purpose that God put us together."

I didn't know, couldn't know, what Joy was going through. She was still processing the depth of her loss. Hershel recently had died, and she left her church after 44 years—so many feelings and emotions were stirred up and surfacing. When Naomi and Ruth decided to stay together during an intense famine, they both went on until they came to Bethlehem. Something bigger than them was about to happen and they didn't know it yet. *When they arrived in Bethlehem, the whole town was stirred about them, and said, Is this Naomi?* (Ru 1:19) Even with all the love and support her family and friends offered, our friendship filled a void at a time in her life when she most needed it.

Joy explained, "Our friendship reminded me that God had provided someone who loved me as much as I loved them, and I needed it so badly because many of my relationships through the years had been flawed in one way or another. I never felt comfortable in a relationship that was just emotional; instead, I had a wonderful spiritual embodiment about it that I can't explain—it's just there, and you know that you are fulfilling for each other God's plan for your lives and the lives of those you touch.

"I had lost my identity. I was a pastor's wife, a minister in my own right, and I was a vital part of so many things. But after 44 years, everything changed overnight.

"Because I felt God wanted me to be strong for my people, I confined my grief so they could share theirs. But instead of experiencing a loving interchange within their grief, fear and insecurity flourished among the flock. The church secretary stepped in front of me, sneered at me, and said, 'You act like you're glad he's gone.' I cried softly, grief stricken by the loss of support that left with the death of my husband.

"I suffered rejection in many areas that were not my fault. My identity was totally gone. I could not go back there and be who I was. The people at the church loved me so much, so I didn't want them to know that the new pastor had told me not to come back because, 'the congregation loves you more than they love me. You cannot come here anymore.'

"Isn't that just awful? Later I confided honestly with another young minister, telling him, 'I don't know who I am. I've lost my identity.' He looked at me and said, 'I have no use for people who talk like that. I have no use for you.' Can you believe that? I was looking for someone to help me understand.

"If there was any time in the world when I needed you, it was right then—I needed our friendship. It felt so good and comfortable. You didn't make demands on me. You didn't make me feel less, or make me feel like I was in danger of being criticized or rejected. It's awful to feel rejection, and I needed somebody to accept and love me.

"So when we met, I felt very comfortable. Our relationship was just right. We could talk about whatever entered our minds, explain and understand the things of God. Our spiritual walk was so real for each of us, and we found some answers together. You were just what I needed."

Our friendship fit. I felt familiar to Joy in her strange new world even though we hardly knew each other. She was like a gold brick that didn't fit anywhere—she had been refined for years but did not fit with the standing masonry. She had so much to give, but when Hershel died, life as she knew it suddenly stopped. She had the need to keep going but didn't know where. God used our mentoring friendship to help fill the voids of a lost love and of a need to belong.

Maria has mentored many women over the years, but when Edith interviewed for the office assistant position, she filled that post and Maria's need for a deep and trusted relationship that lasts to this day. Maria remembers, "From the minute I met Edith I loved her, and I think we both felt an instant comfort in each other's presence. She went with me on a mission trip. When we came back, I was doing a women's retreat, and she accompanied me there as well."

Edith is a talented, professional woman who loved the Lord and wanted a deeper spiritual commitment to Jesus. She wanted meaningful relationships in her life. Maria's calling was to minister to women and to help them fulfill God's calling on their lives. What makes their relationship unique is that Edith now runs Maria's ministry.

Maria needed a strong support system to minister to women around the world. God knew this, so when they met, the two women had a sense God meant for them to support one another. Maria filled Edith's need for love and belonging; Edith filled Maria's need for a talented support system; both of them received deep and meaningful relationship.

"I became like a mother to Edith, and I loved her through a lot of things. We have lived the details of life together. There have been times she's practically lived with me. She's just like my own daughter; I watched her grow until I no longer mentor her. We no longer have that same relationship.

"It was 11 years ago that I started with Edith. We've been through a lot together.

"Edith speaks to God with all her heart. She didn't marry until she was 38, and he is a Godly and wonderful man. Edith now runs the ministry. She is leading her first mission team. I'm going along to head up the ministry, but she's leading the team. And she's doing an exceptional job."

God used Maria to equip Edith to be all He meant her to be. God used Edith to fill the need that Maria had to pass her baton of ministry so that Maria would have peace of mind. This all happened within the context of a deeply meaningful and trusted friendship. Maria mentored Edith. Both were able to be lost in the comfort of a fulfilled friendship. Edith needed this comfort level to feel safe enough to vent her feelings, learn to acknowledge them, and not let them rule her.

According to Edith, "Maria and I met about 11 years ago at church where she was on staff, when I volunteered to help her as an office assistant. We hit it off from the beginning, and we had a wonderful relationship from the beginning.

"It was crazy how much it fit. It was awesome to see.

An exhilarating case from the very beginning, Maria is a very prophetically intuitive person, and I think God contributed to why our friendship went off on such a fast pace. She had a lot of insight, with the ability to see what the Lord saw in me. She knew what I had to deal with in order to become what God meant me to be."

Both Maria and Edith are brilliant, high-energy women, and both have met their match in each other. They went on mission trips around the world answering God's call on their lives through ministry and each other. Edith recalled, "After five trips together, Maria believed the Lord was leading her out of her staff position at the church and into full-time ministry. We noticed we were both moved by the same things: reaching out to people in Third World countries, loving people, and feeling compassion for their needs. We loved the prophetic and seeing where the Lord was taking people, not just where they were but where they were going.

"We became family to each other. She really was a mother to me, so it wasn't just a spiritual mom. It wasn't like a once-a-week meeting with a start and stop time. It was more like we'd have dinner and then go shopping. All of those things that were very integral to our relationship caused it to be more vulnerable emotionally."

Maria and Edith created workable boundaries, making it safe to be spontaneous and vulnerable with each other. Edith tested the integrity of their relationship behind closed doors. She needed to know if Maria would be consistent. She wanted to see if Maria really lived what she said. Because it is easy to see the symptom as the root of the situation, Edith was not conscious of her own heart. "I don't know if I was aware at the time of what the needs were. It wasn't like it was a relationship I was looking for.

"In retrospect, there was a place in me where I was

emotionally stuck. I felt places of real disappointment in people who had been in authority over me. I had a hard time with the whole idea of authority. I had felt disappointed and totally rejected.

"I tested Maria in some ways out of my own emotional immaturity, seeing if she would walk further than a certain point with me. I needed emotional consistency."

God knew Edith was ready for the relationship with Maria, and that Edith was ready for what Maria had. "I think other relationships were wonderful and appropriate at the time, but there was something about my relationship with Maria that just went to a deeper level the Lord intended at that time. I had to cross over into a different emotional dimension to be able to travel the road He wanted me to go. And I don't think I'm done."

Edith was experiencing a deeper emotional and spiritual dimension, which facilitated a deeper spiritual fulfillment and healing by letting her be all that God meant her to be.

"I've been to counseling, and it was right for the time. But this is different. This relationship is one of action. I lived with this person, and the Lord used that to deal with my heart in a different way than when you go to a counselor and just talk to them. It's just a different method I guess.

"Maria took me to the next place with God. She has such a magnanimous nature; you can't stay around her and not be completely motivated to move onto the next level or next thing and reach for the impossible. That's just who she is.

"It's so easy to hide in church, but it is impossible to hide in an intimate relationship. You can go in and out of church and not really rub elbows. You can get involved in things and help here and there, but do you start a relationship like the one that I have with Maria?

Because of the intimacy of the relationship, it causes you to deal with your stuff and go on to a deeper level of maturity and with the Lord."

Maria agrees. "Edith is really coming into her own place designed by God. And I feel like the last horizon, the last territory we are going to take together is the public speaking. Since her fear of abandonment was so strong, it scared her to think that she was called into the ministry, but she is.

"She has her own video production company; she's a very successful woman who does exceptional work. She's in great demand for her videos, and she's beginning to speak. We'll go to Russia together this year. She will be co-speaking with me at the women's retreat, and she will be leading a team. I feel like this is it. Edith is really going to see the true destiny God has on her life.

"You need to evaluate your purpose and what you're doing. Many women in ministry never allow the person they're mentoring to walk alongside them. It's not good because the person who's being mentored finally has to go away to find their peers.

"And then it becomes a control issue. The person who is mentoring is doing so out of a place of insecurity. They don't feel good enough inside themselves to let go and let their former mentor be their peer. When you allow them to be your peer, you now have the help that you've needed so long that you didn't have. I can trust Edith with my life. I never have to worry about her. She runs the ministry; she's my boss. I don't have to worry, 'Does Edith want the best for this ministry? Are her motives pure?' I know who she is. There's trust and integrity there."

Although mentoring makes life more meaningful, God intends mentoring not just to fill each other's needs. Maria felt that was difficult to address. "Here's the deal," she said. "We do take comfort in the person, but the glory goes to God. Because I look at Edith and I think, 'What if I hadn't answered the mandate that God gave me concerning her life?' Where would she be today?

"And would she know the value that she is in the ministry, or would she just be out there floundering in the world now? It's just a great joy to me. This is what I always tell women: 'Don't tell me that you're finding yourself. You find yourself in your relationships.'

"I think our relationships with people are barometers of our relationship with God. If we're in a good relationship with others, that's a good indication that we have a good relationship with God. But if we're in bad relationships, then we have to take a look at ourselves and see what we're doing wrong. That's really what life is about, and that's how we find ourselves—in our relationships."

Through a trusted friendship, just as Maria showed Edith, Joy showed me how to live better principles and how to understand my defining moments so that I could become all God meant me to be. Defining moments don't have to involve a mentor, but mentors can fast track the process, as Joy did for me.

The brutality of her stepfather birthed in Joy the desire to live with purpose. The death of her husband opened up doors she never noticed. She knows it's not about her; it's about God and the people He puts in her path. She showed me that purpose isn't some enigma far away waiting to be discovered, it is already there in front of me in everything I think, feel, do, and say. Purpose is waking up each day and seeing the meaning in everything I do and all God puts in my day. I just have to recognize it and receive it.

The Lord will perfect that which concerns me . . . (Ps 138:8). Joy learned her purpose in life through God's perfecting her in her trials. She recalled, "One time I cried to God and I said, 'Please God, why do I have to go through these awful things? One thing after another and nobody can help me! But God, You will help me I know, but why?'

"And He spoke to my heart clearly, 'Joy, are you better than I am? I was crushed so that I could understand you, and now you want an understanding heart? You cannot understand other people unless you have felt the blows that they feel. I love you, and I'm answering your prayer. I'm giving you an understanding heart by the adversities that come into your life. And yet I give you the victory to overcome them; I give you the pathway to find the answers. You do come through and you will come through because I have a plan for your life. Your life's purpose is wrapped up in me and I will perfect it.' "

God has upheld Joy's life by His Word. *He Who began a good work in you will continue until the day of Jesus Christ [right up to the time of His return] . . .* (Ph 1:6).

'Meant to be' precedes 'meant to do'. If we are who God means us to be, then doing what God wants us to do will follow naturally. We want you to experience and embrace a deeper sense of connectedness with the most significant relationships in your life.

Defining moments are those times in our lives when circumstances or our feelings about them are so outstanding that we know the choices we are being given in that instant will define who we are and determine our destiny. They reveal your purpose and show your worth.

You *know* you have to answer the question, "What am I going to do about this?" Like the eye of a perfect storm, a defining moment is the pinnacle of converging circumstances and related feelings that determine the outcome of one's fate.

My dad always worked a lot. My husband has always worked a lot. And I too worked a lot—at feeling at sorry for myself.

While I was pregnant with our second child, my husband Michael was fund-raising for Pat Robertson's presidential campaign. Every time he would get on another flight, I wanted to cry. I felt tired, insignificant, and overwhelmed. I reached the end of my rope, and it was a pivotal time. This defining moment revealed my purpose in such a wonderful way through Joy.

"I feel so miserable and awful!" I tearfully told Joy, words and emotions overflowing. She listened quietly with her heart and understood.

"It's difficult being the wind under the wings," Joy thoughtfully replied. That defining moment impacted my life forever and showed my worth as a person, not as an extension of someone else. *He . . . brings forth the wind from His treasuries* (Je 51:16). What meant the most was understanding and receiving God's love for me when I felt like an invisible, worthless wind. *Bless (affectionately, gratefully praise) the Lord, O my soul! O Lord my God, You are very great! You are clothed with honor and majesty—[You are the One] Who . . . makes winds His messengers, flames of fire His ministers* (Ps 104:1-2,4). It gave meaning to the circumstances and feelings that followed. Joy accepted being the wind under wings in her capacity as a pastor's wife. We both learned the wind can become a hurricane when necessary.

Her simple words validated my existence and enlightened everything in that moment. I wasn't giving myself enough credit for taking care of my children and making our house a home. My role was just as vital as my husband's.

The encouragement, love, and understanding she shared inspired me to make constructive choices about the situation and understand the learning curve that I was in. In choosing God's way over my way, I was learning to let Him be my Higher Power instead of my husband. I was expecting Michael to fill a void in my heart, but Joy's mentoring taught me that only God is capable of such Sovereignty.

Sometimes events in our past can be so overwhelming we cannot cope with them. God gives us these moments. *And though the Lord gives you the bread of adversity and the water of affliction, yet your Teacher will not hide Himself any more, but your eyes will constantly behold your Teacher. And your ears will hear a word behind you, saying, This is the way; walk in it, when you turn to the right hand and when you turn to the left* (Is 30:20-21). We compartmentalize our thoughts and feelings about what happens, and like a broken toy put on a shelf to fix later, we hide our emotions. Those events represent the defining moments which reveal our purpose.

Rachel had a defining moment when she chose to recommit herself to the Lord. When she was eight years old, she asked Jesus into her heart and loved going to Sunday school even though her family did not. Her mom sent her anyway, and Jesus filled her heart with His love. He gave her the motivation she needed to do well in school even through the pain of her parents' divorce. Then the unconscionable happened—her father was murdered—and it was more than Rachel could bear. How could Jesus love her and let this happen?

The seed of hatred seemed to grow in every aspect of Rachel's life. Her job, friends, family, living conditions—everything got worse. She was sitting on the floor, broken and in the darkest mire of her life, when she cried out to Him. "Jesus! Jesus!" she begged. "I can't take it anymore. I can't stand it. Take me. Take all of me, and make me Yours! I need You to change everything—job, home, friends . . . everything!"

In that moment, Rachel felt a calming presence she had not experienced in years. The tornado that ripped through her soul was replaced by the healing of the Holy Spirit, slowly setting her free forever. When Rachel calls me, I listen. God meant for Rachel and me to be friends.

> *Lord, You will ordain peace (God's favor and blessings, both temporal and spiritual) for us, for You have also wrought in us and for us all our works. O Lord, our God, other masters besides You have ruled over us, but we will acknowledge and mention Your name only. They [the former tyrant masters] are dead, they shall not live and reappear; they are powerless ghosts, they shall not rise and come back. Therefore You have visited and made an end of them and caused every memory of them [every trace of their supremacy] to perish.*
>
> Isaiah 26:12-14

A mentor gives you the skills and coping tools needed to make wise decisions about your defining moments. Rachel appreciates that I am a human voice with God's words. Although you can't go back in time and change the past, you can always change your choices and perspective about the past.

Mentors are people you gravitate toward because they have what you need. Joy made some outstanding choices in spite of and because of incredible odds. The story of Joy's defining moments and the choices she made show her purpose, the depth of her wisdom, and the power of free will. And this is what she passed on to me.

The year was 1918 and as World War I was ending in Europe, baby Joy was born in Cain Hill, Arkansas. Only six weeks old when she moved with her parents to Oklahoma, they eventually settled on a little farm nestled in the foothills of a small agricultural community.

Life was abundant with love, home-cooked meals, and siblings to play with. Joy's parents adored her. They not only passed on their love for her but also their love for Jesus, which became the cornerstone of her life. She did not realize how much that love would be challenged by the hate that would later enter her heart.

Spark of Divinity

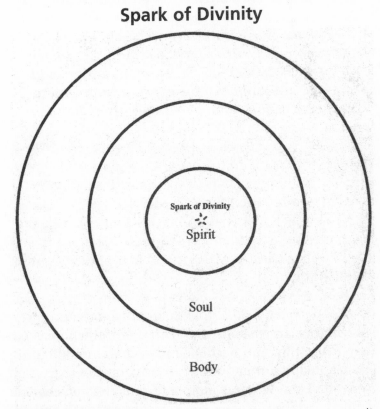

Spark of Divinity: Dwells in your Spirit or your innermost man. It is a God-instilled sense of greatness you are born with. It is of God and not of you. That's why it's always there.

Joy's mother was her mentor, an avid listener and a source of great validation for Joy. She passed her love for Jesus to Joy and ignited Joy's spark of divinity. The spark of divinity is God's little spark of life in each human being.

God created us with three dimensions: spirit (the innermost man), soul (the inner man), and body (the outer man). God's spark of divinity is in the innermost man. *May He grant you out of the rich treasury of His glory to be strengthened and reinforced with mighty power in the inner man by the [Holy] Spirit [Himself indwelling your innermost being and personality]* (Ep 3:16).

The spark won't go away or change because it is not about you. It is of God and is always there, waiting to be uncovered, ignited, and burnt brightly. God will use anything to call forth the spark in you, sometimes through mentoring and sometimes through the circumstances of life.

Joy learned from her mother that *listening feels like love* or *listen with your heart.* This principle of listening with her heart later became the hallmark of Joy's counseling ministry as a pastor's wife.

Her mother heard Joy, and Joy knew it. If something became a burden in her heart, she knew she could tell her mother without any fear of judgment or condemnation.

Once, when she was older, Joy wanted to go to a dance. "It was on a Friday night," she reminisced, "with a friend who hung out with a crowd who moved faster than I was used to. When I told Mother about it, she listened and then asked me two questions: 'Honey, how would you feel telling your Sunday school friends about this dance?'

"I said nothing. Mother continued, 'Are these people friends you enjoy being with?'

"I paused, pondering the answers to the questions she put forth. She looked at me and smiled. 'I know you'll use good judgment.' She let it go, and I decided to stay home." Because she always felt listened to and affirmed by her mother, Joy learned how to own her decisions.

The year 1929 brought the stock market crash, the death of her father, and an end to the life Joy knew. She was only eleven but remembers well his long battle to overcome double pneumonia and an abscessed lung without the benefit of antibiotics.

In the final days of his illness, relatives and neighbors came to their house to comfort and assist in any way they could. He was critical now, and the minutes seemed like hours as he lay there dying. Gentle hands ushered Joy and her siblings to his bedside while he breathed his last laborious breath . . . each one farther and farther apart. Then he was gone. Her daddy was gone! The daddy who held her on his lap, warmed her little feet in the winter by the old pot-bellied stove, told her Bible stories about Jesus, took her to town with him in the old spring wagon, and beamed with pride when she spoke her recitation in the school program. How she missed her father's love, his smell, his warm laugh, his strength, his reassurance!

Poverty stripped Joy of all security, as these years proved to be more than Joy's mother could bear with three children. They sold the family farm, and Joy's mother met Thomas, a successful businessman who seemed to love the family. His surface charm faded faster than the wedding bells. Once the ceremony was over, the nightmare began for Joy and her siblings. He loved Ollie, Joy's mother, but he loathed the children. Unspeakable abuse became a way of life for many years. Yet, it was this time of turbulent brutality that birthed in Joy an unquenchable longing to help people.

The memory of her father's love was quickly becoming a faded movie in Joy's young mind. Being born into a Christian family, she treasured the unconditional love lavished upon her by her Mommy and Daddy when she was small.

Now that her father was gone, Joy assumed many adult responsibilities as the oldest child in her family. She was used to watching out for her mother and her siblings, but her caretaking abilities were challenged by her new stepfather's erratic behavior.

Joy resisted, and respectfully disputed him to his dismay, refusing to let him step all over her family. So when she resisted this new man in the family, he directed his rage toward her.

She lived with the knowledge that at any moment he could snap, and her life would be over. As time went on, she believed he would to kill her. Joy pleaded with her mother to leave this man.

Torn between her intense love and loyalty to her daughter and the need to provide for her dependent family, Joy's mother struggled to protect Joy and to reason with her daughter. While so many others were going without, they had a home to live in, food on the table, and clothes on their backs. With his reputable job at the Conoco Oil Company, the family was financially secure during the Depression. So Joy endured his unpredictable behavior and his predictable beatings, wondering what would happen next.

Then one day without warning, the big hit came. During a dispute, her stepfather crossed the invisible line of physical civility, unbridling his hatred toward Joy like never before. The bottom of his huge hand swung so hard against her small, 13-year-old head that he knocked Joy down, rupturing her eardrum. It cost

Joy her hearing in her right ear. When the doctor questioned her about what happened, she hid the truth. After all, her stepfather was an upstanding church man in the community; she had to protect her family.

This repugnant man's insane jealousy of Joy was always simmering at the top, ready to boil over. Unconsciously, he knew he couldn't compete with Ollie's love for Joy. He showed contempt instead of compassion when Joy doubled over in pain, not knowing what it was, then straightened out. Her mother called the doctor.

After examining Joy, the doctor took her mother and stepfather into the room and told them, "She has had an acute attack of appendicitis. The appendix has ruptured and that's why she straightened out. If she doesn't get help within the next few hours, there's not much hope. She'll die."

Her stepfather towered ominously over Joy's petite frame. His anger spread across his monstrous face like a red rash. With trembling lips he snarled, "Well then, she can just die."

At three o'clock in the morning, a doctor in a drunken stupor operated on Joy. He put a tube in her side. She remembers waking up with her mother at her bedside, hearing the nurses whisper to each other, "It's too bad this little girl has to die."

"Mother," murmured Joy, scarcely conscious, "am I going to die?"

With big tears rolling down her face, her mother replied more confidently than she felt, "Honey, we hope not. Jesus is looking over you."

Joy survived. Her recovery was slow, her health weak, but her vengeance and hatred toward her stepfather were healthier than ever. The dark clouds of reproach dimmed Joy's spark of divinity, leaving only a smoldering little wick.

Her tenacity was a quality that worked both for her

and against her. It may have catalyzed her stepfather's rage toward her, but it also saved her life and kept her going. She was relentless with her mother, imploring her regularly to divorce that awful man.

Perhaps Joy understood that her mother's intense love for her was so great, she really did consider divorce during the Depression, but knew ultimately it was not in her family's best interests. Unfortunately, Joy could not believe that, and she tenaciously kept talking with her mother, trying to convince her.

Reproach will take its toll on you spiritually, mentally, and physically. Following its dictates, Joy was so bound by contempt toward her stepfather that she once cried three days straight, imploring her mother to leave him.

Her insatiable desire for vengeance was like a dry well demanding a downpour. Finally, at the end of the third tearful day, she announced to her mother with unshakable resolution, "Mother, if you don't divorce that man, I am going to poison him!"

Her mother stared at her, astonished and speechless. She didn't know what to say, fearing the consequences. Her daughter had a strong track record of following through on what she said. Joy dried her hot tears, pushed back her powerful emotions, straightened her shoulders, and stomped out of the room with absolute intent. What neither knew at this place in time was that they were both currently in the eye of the storm that was defining Joy's destiny. She truly wanted to poison her cruel stepfather.

But just as Joy was about to go marching off to the medicine cabinet, she took a turn toward her bedroom instead, got down on her knees, and with outstretched arms cried out, "Oh, God, please help me. Help me! Give me an understanding heart so I can help other people, so they won't have to hurt like I do." This defining moment revealed her purpose more clearly than anything else ever had. A new strength surged through Joy's young soul. She knew it was a decision coupled with a strong emotion and intent. She knew what she was going to do. Her choice of good over evil had determined her destiny.

Joy responded the way she did because the love she had in her heart was greater than the hate that had threatened to usurp its place. Her defining moment reflected her purpose and showed her worth.

Although she knew God had heard her impassioned plea, forgiveness was a road filled with obstacles and pitfalls that would take years to follow. However, this was all part of the forgiveness process, and Joy chose God's will over her way, slowly thawing her emotions that had been frozen in fear.

The shadow of her cruel stepfather loomed long after Joy left home and married Hershel. She couldn't pardon him for all the years of battering she'd endured. Even after coming into a pleasant place of love and peace in her marriage with Hershel, Joy stayed in touch with her beloved mother, with the threatening presence of her stepfather never far away.

Once when visiting, he tried to hit Joy, but she looked at him and declared, "Oh no, you won't hit me. I'm not under your roof. I'm not under your hand. You put your hand down! You're not going to hit me."

She knew reproach was holding her back, but Joy didn't know what to do about it. So she made it a matter of prayer, "Oh, God, I just don't know what to do. I know I'm not supposed to hate my stepfather, but I do. I hate him with all my heart. He deserves to go to hell, and frankly, God, I hope he does. Please, please, You have to help me."

She didn't whine and complain to other people . . . she went straight to God. Over and over Joy pleaded in prayer for help, even feeling like she might go to Hell herself. Finally one day, the thought came to her from God, "Joy, have you ever thought he really is pitiful? That he really is going to hell?"

It was a defining moment that revealed her purpose. She made her choice. True unconditional forgiveness was born in Joy's heart at that pivotal time. This defining moment reinforced Joy's choice made years before—to help people. A new realization dawned that Joy had not seen before. Yes, her stepfather deserved hell, but as a sinner so did she and she didn't want to go where he was going. Then compassion quietly entered, and Joy started to see the pain and torment that had taunted such a troubled man for so many years. A man can't give what he doesn't have, so her stepfather was unable to provide Joy and her siblings the love they desperately needed.

Joy had been to hell and back with him, but for her it was past. For her stepfather, it was still an ongoing torture.

After Joy's mother died, he endured long, lonely hours by himself interrupted occasionally by family visits. Joy knew what she was supposed to do, but she had to get her heart to cooperate.

Hershel's invitation to take her stepfather to a baseball game was only accepted on the condition that Joy joined them. By now he was old and feeble, and more unlovable than ever. Begrudgingly, Joy agreed, not knowing she was about to enter another situation that would change her life forever.

In the living room, Joy sat as far from her stepfather as possible. He got up trembling with age, his once big body now brittle and bent over. He slowly shuffled into the next room and returned, holding a crumbly piece of typewritten paper.

With gnarled, shaking hands, her stepfather

passed the paper to Joy, asking her to *please* read it. "What's the matter with this? The man doesn't even know how to write a story on a piece of paper," she sarcastically thought to herself.

The paper was titled, "Love." Joy's criticism flowed effortlessly and smoothly. "Sure he knows all about this. I'm going to read something wonderful here."

Instead, his words rocked her foundation, taking her by complete surprise. They formed thoughts and feelings Joy never knew existed in his soul.

"When I was a young man, I married my first wife and had two children by her, and I loved them. When she died, I married Ollie and I loved her, but I did not love her three children. I did not know I was supposed to. In the years that followed, I became indebted to Joy, because Joy was kinder to me than my own children."

Joy's mind flashed back to an almost forgotten memory. At one time her stepfather was going to shoot and kill his own son. Joy's mother stood between the gun in his hand and his son and evenly declared, "If you shoot him, you will have to shoot me first."

Her stepfather continued, "Now I am an old man; I'm sick and nobody loves me. I need forgiveness. I need somebody to love me and forgive me."

Joy's caustic thoughts bit back, "You bet you do!"

Like the sinner dying on the cross next to Jesus went from mocking Him to begging for mercy, so Joy went from hating him to understanding who her stepfather really was. She looked into his despondent eyes and tears streamed down her face. He too, was crying uncontrollably.

She didn't know what to do, but she had to do something. Answering her prayer, God was using this defining moment to reveal her purpose to help others. She got up from her seat, walked over to where he was, knelt in front of him, took his pitiful bony hands in hers, looked up into his face weathered by life's battles, and did the very best she could at that time. "Oh, Tom, if anyone could write anything as wonderful as that, they can't be all bad." In that moment, forgiveness became a reality.

Soft winds of mercy gently blew away the dark, stormy clouds which had shrouded Joy's spirit for so long. The process of forgiveness was complete, settling into her soul, never to leave, only to strengthen. But what do we do when death or circumstances prevent face-to-face forgiveness?

Rachel was only 14 years old when another man took her father's life. How could this happen to her? How could something so terrible and violent be so close to her? How could Jesus love her and let this happen? During that time, a seed of hatred took root. She felt justified in hating the man who took her dad from her. For the next 17 years, her hatred spread like a cancer taking hold in all areas of her life until it brought her to a place of complete brokenness before God.

This defining moment directed God's purposes for Rachel. Just as Elijah feared God on His mountain and was relieved that *the Lord was not in the fire; and after the fire [a sound of gentle stillness and] a still, small voice* (1 Ki 19:12), she heard God's still voice say, "Forgive him."

"What??" Rachel thought. "Forgive my father's killer?"

"Forgive him, and ask him to forgive you for the hatred in your heart."

God's still, small voice was getting too loud for Rachel. This was asking an exorbitant amount!

Her emotions screamed one thing, but the peace in her spirit said another. "OK, Lord. I don't want to, but if this is really what You want me to do, then I will."

She wrote a letter to her father's murderer, forgiving him and asking him to forgive her for the hatred in her heart. When Rachel dropped the envelope into the mailbox, all the hatred held in her heart went with the letter. Shortly after, she left for a ten-day mission trip to Thailand. An unusual note awaited her return to the United States. Her father's killer responded with an amazing letter forgiving her and thanking her for forgiving him. He is still in prison but had committed his life to Jesus. Rachel is free from the prison of hatred her soul was in.

This was not the end of Rachel's path of forgiveness. During her Biblical Counseling Foundations course, she knew she had to face a past trauma and forgive the perpetrator. She was only three years old when her uncle sexually molested her. He died during the time she was taking the course, so God used this to put her in a special place of healing and forgiveness. She faced all the unresolved anger she held, and her forgiveness set her free. With the help of a strong spiritual friend, she sat down with her cousin, her uncle's son.

Rachel expressed the anger, pain, and shame she felt. Then she forgave her uncle through his son who accepted his father's actions and Rachel's forgiveness. Rachel was set free from victimization. She is now the victor, waking up each day and living out God's purpose as He puts it before her, comforting those with the comfort she has received.

Personal Process Assessment

Defining moments reveal your purpose. A defining moment is a moment of impact when you make decisions that show who you are and what your purpose is. Purpose is waking up every day, seeing meaning in everything God puts before you, and understanding the repercussions of your choices. Destructive choices will have detrimental consequences that conceal who you are. Constructive choices have positive results that will reveal who you are meant to be. Regardless of your choices, these moments define you. What are your defining moments? Are you being inspired or incited by these pivotal points in time?

We want you to quietly ask yourself and ask God to reveal to you significant events in your life. God uses these defining moments to give you gifts. He gave you all that is already in you; future gifts come to fruition through your experiences.

Mentoring clarifies our defining moments. Defining moments often need wisdom. As a young mother I felt like my life wasn't important, but Joy created an image in my mind showing where I was, the setting I was really in, and the future to come so that I had a clear perspective and a renewed purpose. Mentoring illuminates these moments in our life that impact us and gives us the wisdom we need to make mature decisions based on what we experience. Who has helped you understand your defining moments? Who are you helping? How are they the catalysts to fulfilling your life's purpose?

You can't go anywhere without forgiveness. Joy had to forgive her stepfather. I had to forgive myself. Who do you have to forgive? Because forgiveness is so vital, the following prayer is provided to give you a chance to either start the process of forgiveness, or thoroughly forgive whoever you need to.

———◆━◆◆◆━◆———

"Heavenly Father, in Jesus' Name, thank you for creating (name of person or even yourself) in Your image. With Your help, and with all my heart, I forgive _____ for not becoming all You created him or her to be. I realize now that _____ needed the healing that I am now receiving. Someway and somehow as I accept and forgive _____, may their (or my) life be all You ever meant it to be. Help me to forgive _____ all his or her offenses against me. I accept _____ as an unhealed and needy person. There but for Your grace go I. Thank You for all You created _____ to be, even when I fail to see it. Give me eyes to see. I will look for the real person You intended _____ to be and affirm it whenever I see it. I look to You now for the love and affirmation I always wanted so badly from _____. Love _____ through me in Jesus' Name. Amen.

———◆━◆◆◆━◆———

One must imitate God's own way of dealing with the soul, softening His rebuke, so that the person rebuffed feels as if it was rather self-reproach, and a sense of wounded love, than God rebuking. All other methods of guidance, reproving impatiently, or because one is vexed at infirmities, smack of earthly judgments, not the correction of grace. The greater our own self-love, the more severe critics we shall be. The less self love we have, the more we know how to adapt ourselves to curing our neighbor's failings of that kind; we learn better never to lance without putting plenty of healing ointment to the wound, never to purge the patient without feeding him up, never to risk an operation save when nature indicates its safety. One learns to wait years before giving a salutary warning to wait till Providence prepares suitable external circumstances and grace opens the heart. If you persist in gathering fruit before it is ripe, you simply waste your labor.

François de Salignac de la Mothe-Fénelon

So Elijah left there and found Elisha son of Shaphat, whose plowing was being done with twelve yoke of oxen, and he drove the twelfth. Elijah crossed over to him and cast his mantle upon him. He left the oxen and ran after Elijah and said, Let me kiss my father and mother, and then I will follow you. And he [testing Elisha] said, Go on back. What have I done to you? [Settle it for yourself.] So Elisha went back from him. Then he took a yoke of oxen, slew them, boiled their flesh with the oxen's yoke [as fuel], and gave to the people, and they ate. Then he arose, followed Elijah, and served him.

1 Kings 19:19-21

That is why I would remind you to stir up (rekindle the embers of, fan the flame of, and keep burning) the [gracious] gift of God, [the inner fire] that is in you by means of the laying on of my hands [with those of the elders at your ordination].

2 Timothy 1:6

CHAPTER THREE
Seeing God in Our Friendships

"Again I tell you, if two of you on earth agree (harmonize together, make a symphony together) about whatever [anything and everything] they may ask, it will come to pass and be done for them by My Father in heaven. For wherever two or three are gathered (drawn together as My followers) in (into) My name, there I AM in the midst of them."

Matthew 18:19-20

Hold fast and follow the pattern of wholesome and sound teaching which you have heard from me, in [all] the faith and love which are [for us] in Christ Jesus.

2 Timothy 1:13

Rings and jewels are not gifts, but apologies for gifts. The only gift is a portion of thyself.

Ralph Waldo Emerson

Joy mentored me through friendship. Who are your mentoring friends? We needed each other, filled a void in each other, and wanted our relationship. There is cohesiveness, a joining and feeling of mutual blessing and contribution that fuels our camaraderie, keeping it dynamic and alive.

In Greek mythology, Mentor was the loyal friend and advisor of Odysseus. Mentor went on to teach Telemachus, the son of Odysseus. He was a trusted friend before he taught. Mentoring is a principle when it is the cause of learning. It becomes a process when in the friendship it grows into the way of learning.

Joy and I enjoy a friendship that is so fulfilling that learning and receiving wisdom is just a natural consequence of the commitment we have to each other. Both of us has an innate need to give and receive love and aid that can only be filled by this process.

We are kindred spirits, cut from the same cloth. We intuitively know we are safe with each other, and we share a candid and spontaneous bond.

This sort of relationship is nothing new. From the beginning of time, God has passed the blessing of mentoring when He breathed His breath of life into humanity. It is His nature to give life, and He made our nature likewise.

When Mary Poppins said, "Just a spoonful of sugar helps the medicine go down," she could have been referring to mentoring. I've learned so many life lessons in such a fun way, I wasn't even consciously aware of it.

Although life has its ups and downs, there is a clear path of peace and well-being you can stay on regardless of your circumstances. Joy passed this place of peace on to me through her life by opening the door to the innermost chambers of her heart and letting me in within the snug setting of our deep-seated friendship.

Let all men know and perceive and recognize your unselfishness (your considerateness, your forbearing spirit). The Lord is near [He is coming soon]. Do not fret or have any anxiety about anything, but in every circumstance and in everything, by prayer and petition (definite requests), with thanksgiving, continue to make your wants known to God. And God's peace [shall be yours, that tranquil state of a soul assured of its salvation through Christ, and so fearing nothing from God and being content with its earthly lot of whatever sort that is, that peace] which transcends all understanding shall garrison and mount guard over your hearts and minds in Christ Jesus. For the rest, brethren, whatever is true, whatever is worthy of reverence and is honorable and seemly, whatever is just, whatever is pure, whatever is lovely and lovable, whatever is kind and winsome and gracious, if there is any virtue and excellence, if there is anything worthy of praise, think on and weigh and take account of these things [fix your minds on them]. Practice what you have learned and received and heard and seen in me, and model your way of living on it, and the God of peace (of untroubled, undisturbed well-being) will be with you.

Philippians 4:5-9

As I practice what Joy does, my peace strengthens.

Mentoring is neither training nor parenting. After giving birth four times, it is my personal experience and belief that God puts an instinctive love in most mothers the minute that baby is born. This may not hold true given severe dysfunction or trauma. My mom would do anything for me and instilled in me a deep sense of love and belonging. She was loving and nurturing, wise, and caring. Mom trained me up in the way I should go, and as I grew older, I came back to the path for which she prepared me.

She instructed me in such a way to bring a desired condition or behavior. She was a wonderful stay-at-home mother who taught me well.

She taught me some of the most delicious Italian

dishes passed down from her mother. So authentic you'd never find them in a restaurant here in the United States. My children love it when they enter our home and smell garlic simmering in olive oil because they know something good is cooking.

Mom passed on all in her life to me as God gave it to her, and I do the same with my children. Mom's greatest gift to me was passing on a spiritual sense of well-being that everything happens the way God meant it to, so don't worry. Parenting is subjective and offers the best setting to raise children; mentoring is objective and offers the best setting to mature adults.

Mentoring in its nature is objective and offers the best setting to mature adults. The crossover appeal is whatever lessons I didn't or refused to learn when young; mentoring offers me another chance to learn my lesson. As adults, there are areas in our lives where we still act as children in adult bodies and simply need a safe setting to mature and heal.

Jennifer Cecil is a spirit-filled counselor who loves Jesus and integrates her spirituality and faith in her counseling practice. Her niece Hilary Griffith is 19 years old and on a full academic scholarship to Arizona State University.

When Hilary was raped, her pain became her mother's pain and it was an unbearable load for Hilary to carry. "My family's always been very close. Every summer, we take trips together, and we do little family get-togethers all year. My aunt Jen and I have always had a pretty good relationship. But after the rape happened, my entire family was devastated.

"It was really difficult to talk to my mom about it—both my parents actually—just because it was really hard for me to see how much it hurt them to find out how I was doing. If I was doing badly, then they would be upset, and I didn't want that. So I'd tell them I was doing fine even if I wasn't just to save them the pain.

"Jen was there for me from the beginning. That night she was there in the hospital with my family, and she was calling to check on me and offered to take me out to coffee and just talk and be there for me. So we started meeting, and she'd ask how I was and just be there."

Both Hilary and her aunt Jennifer understand God put them together to fulfill His purposes in their lives. They experienced a deep sense of spiritual fulfillment and understanding that has matured them both and brought great healing and deliverance for Hilary.

Mentoring is counseling for the calling. In our loyal friendship, God used Joy to prepare me for the road He intended. I needed her wisdom and experience to be spiritually equipped to effectively serve in the capacity God had designed for me.

Mentoring is not coaching. Coaching is training for a specific outcome. Mentoring is rooted in friendship. Coaching transfers knowledge and expertise, although it may evolve into a mentored relationship. Only mentoring is rooted in a trusted friendship within a spiritual setting.

Ruth responded to God's calling through her relationship with Naomi. Widowed and without children, they were truly desperate housewives! But when Naomi encouraged Ruth to go find a life for herself, Ruth chose to stay with Naomi. *And Ruth said, Urge me not to leave you or to turn back from following you; for where you go I will go, and where you lodge I will lodge. Your people shall be my people and your God my God* (Ru 1:16).

Both were called by God, but Naomi, an Israelite, had a deep-seated faith while Ruth, a Moabite, came from a people with a reputation for being wild and without God. Ruth really loved God and wanted to follow Him but had to learn how. Naomi and Ruth had a spiritual tie and ultimately a calling of God on Ruth's life that she instinctively knew and was responding to.

Mentoring implies *choice* and *change*. My two younger children have had the same wonderful first-grade teacher. Christine is a pretty, young, energetic woman with an incredibly positive and loving way with the children, yet she exudes an authority beyond her years.

On a field trip, she casually mentioned something about her mother being a first-grade teacher. "No wonder you're so good with the children," I remarked. Her mother was her mentor, a trusted and loyal advisor. Christine may have been born with certain predisposed qualities that would enable her to teach, but she *chose* to act on these pre-determined characteristics, learn from her mother, and make the most of them.

Mentoring is a key ingredient to administering an effective recovery program. In 12-step recovery, we call it "sponsorship." I like doing things "by the book," so when I realized my own need for Al Anon, I figured it would work best if I did what I was supposed to do which included finding a sponsor. So I prayerfully and carefully found someone who seemed to be working the program herself, which she was. The program has a life of its own where peace eventually took place of the chaos inside my own soul.

Relationships of accountability are developed to replace old, dysfunctional habits with healthy, new ones. Within the confines of a trusted friendship, a sponsor passes experience, strength, and hope to the newcomer.

Mentoring, like sponsorship, provides constructive solutions to complex life problems. Sometimes I feel caught in a situation I can't respond to because I can't see the forest for the trees. My sponsor offers real solutions that worked for her; some of them may work for me.

Finding a sponsor who shares the same value system is preferable. There are many people from all ages, professions, and ethnicities. For years, Rachel sought the help of a counselor who did not share her value system. She developed a non-Christian view of healing, flavored with new age perspective. Rachel now understands that true healing can only come from Jesus. If we seek non-Christian mentors, they will lean toward the world's view on healing which is self-help, self-talk, self-control . . . all of which fails in the end because of the reliance on the flawed, human "self."

Alexandra believes part of the problem for professional Christian women is the church's tradition that limits women in ministry. "Here's what I know from being in the ministry for so many years. Church leaders get together, and they do all this stuff, but they don't ever invite the women in the Christian community who are in business and are leaders in their communities—Christian leaders.

"And I thought, 'Oh my goodness, they could teach us so much because sometimes in the church we get into so much unhealthiness. These women who are out in the world, they have learned a professionalism that we need to understand. I think Christian women in business learn to integrate their spirituality into the world around them, while in ministry we tend to stay in this little bubble. We need to learn from them.

"And we need to encourage them. When I was on staff as a women's minister at my church, I used to think, 'The people who are least reached in the church are the professional women.' Why are we not reaching them? Professional women find outlets outside the church, and those women may be of more value on a board than some of the men."

As a result of Alexandra's worldwide ministry, countless professional Christian women have mentored friendships and enjoy deeper spiritual fulfillment with a greater understanding of God's purpose in their lives.

Finding quality counseling takes time, but God provides what we need when we need it. It is important that whomever you learn from is working to stay accountable to God. God doesn't want us to hide behind the Bible or use our Christianity like alcohol. I chose someone who is married with children because our common values will be the most productive way for me to learn and for my sponsor to impart wisdom.

The rooms of my 12-step recovery groups are filled with people coming from many diverse backgrounds and moral systems, but when we walk into the room, we work together for the same principles of living. This is the premise upon which we find our common ground and encourage each other.

It is the same as church; we all have different value systems. We all come from different walks of life, but we share the same desire: to know and love Jesus and each other in a deeper and more meaningful way.

Joy was a safe place to run when I needed wisdom and advice. I instinctively knew I could trust her. Finding someone with whom you feel safe is paramount. If you don't feel safe, you won't confide or confess. No one understands this better than Jennifer and her niece Hilary.

Hilary had a job at a radio station, was active in church, and had a very loving family and boyfriend. A baton twirler for her high school, she's competed all her life, including in the Miss Arizona pageant twice.

On November 9, 2004, her life changed forever. Hilary was in the workout room at her apartment complex, exercising and tanning to get ready for the Miss Scottsdale Pageant. She finished about 9:00 p.m., walked home to her apartment, entered, and locked the door. She went in to take a shower and get ready for bed. As she stepped out, a man who had broken in through the window put a towel over her head.

For the next 45 minutes he raped her. While she was being raped, she heard God's voice tell her she was to forgive this man's actions. Hilary knew Jesus as her Savior and Lord and had a peace that if she died, she'd be in Heaven. As horrific as it was, she cannot imagine the terror of such trauma coupled with not knowing where you would go if you died. Because of her certainty, she was able to surrender the outcome of what happened. The attacker fled when her roommates returned.

That night in the hospital after the police and doctors left, Jennifer stayed. Hilary slept the next couple of days and tried to reorient herself. Jennifer remembered, "Hilary's sister saw her pageant items in the corner of her room and suggested keeping them all together in case she decided to compete in the pageant four days later.

"We all thought there was no way this girl was going to compete—it was a pretty bad assault. After a few days in a daze, she tried to decide whether to even attempt to compete. She went to her coach a couple of times to practice her routine, and her mother told the pageant coordinator Hilary would miss the first evening.

"I remember Hilary calling Thursday night and talking about whether she should compete in the pageant on Saturday. I told her that if she wanted to try but couldn't, it would be fine because no one expected her to compete. The significant part of that conversation was when we prayed. We prayed for God's will, not what Hilary wanted, not what the rest of us wanted, but what God wanted for Hilary.

"She woke up the next morning and decided to compete, and she won Miss Scottsdale. We couldn't believe it. When the judges interviewed Hilary behind the scenes, she introduced herself and said, 'I'm really glad to be here. I wasn't sure I was going to make it— Tuesday night I was raped at knifepoint in my apartment, and I wasn't even sure I would live, much less be here. But I'm here. If I didn't compete, I would let this person destroy my life, and I'm not willing to do that. I'm here to take on the responsibilities of Miss Scottsdale and answer any questions you have for me.' Hilary was able to speak to those judges with authority. It wasn't 'poor me; feel sorry for me.' She did beautifully throughout the entire evening. We were in tears and beside ourselves when she won.

"What she told me later made everything clear. 'Hilary, why did you decide to compete?'

"'Well, Jen, I wasn't sure until I talked to you on the phone.'

"'What was it about that conversation that was meaningful?'

"'You said, "Hilary, I wasn't planning on going to watch you compete, but if you're going to compete I wouldn't miss it for the world.'

"Hilary said that comment turned her around because she knew she had enough support to do it. That amazed me because I thought the significant part was the prayer I had said. But it wasn't—it was support that strengthened her to compete and win. She was relying on my belief in her.

"It's funny that God would use something so seemingly benign. It seemed like pretty normal family support to me, but I suppose God spoke in some way that was audible only to her. Going from the depths of despair Tuesday night to total disbelief and elation Saturday night, this young lady decided to take her life back. Even though she was victimized, she was not going to be a victim. She was the victor."

Hilary intuitively knew she was safe with her aunt. Jennifer gave her the encouragement she needed to overcome so much in such a short time and be who God meant her to be. Hilary needed Jennifer, and Jennifer needed Hilary to fulfill God's call in their lives. Hilary's win was a victory for them both.

Love, wisdom, and communication need to flow freely both ways. Joy knew I needed her, and Joy needed to be needed. We felt safe with each other, respected each other's value systems, and knew we would fill each other's needs. Maslow's Hierarchy of Needs* is a basic psychological profile of the order in which our human needs are met. Our basic needs must be filled before our aesthetic needs can be developed. Jesus knew this, and it is why He healed the sick and fed the hungry first. Then He could save our souls.

Although I disagree with Maslow's premise that humans are basically trustworthy, I do agree with his idea that humans tend toward growth and love. The five levels, starting at the bottom, are physiology, safety, love, esteem, and self-actualization. God used Joy to meet my basic needs so I could self-actualize by becoming who He meant me to be.

Hilary needed the comfort of her trusted relationship with Jen. All of Hilary's family, including Jennifer who had her own practice, encouraged Hilary to seek counseling. "I gave her the name of two people and strongly encouraged her to go and begin talking. She did not want to go to counseling since she didn't know

---

* *Abraham Maslow first published his well-known "Hierarchy of Needs" in his book* Motivation and Personality *(1943). More information can be found online at http://www.deepermind.com/20maslow.htm.*

the women, and she felt like this was such a touchy
subject to discuss with a total stranger. She felt that
she would 'perform' by giving them the answers they
wanted to hear. It's good that she knows herself well
enough to understand she'd perform as she does in
pageants. She's very poised, verbal, and articulate.

"So she went twice to two different counselors, and
her response was, 'Jen, they just sit there. They don't
say anything, and there are these long, pregnant
pauses. They can't tell me anything I don't already
know. I want to talk to you.'

"I explained to her, 'There's this thing called a dual
relationship. Therapists are not allowed to have more
than one relationship with a client. Ethically, I am not
allowed to counsel a family member. I'm too close to
you, so it will not work.'

"Hilary was insistent that she did not want to see
anybody else. So I said, 'OK, Hilary, I will not counsel
you, but I will meet with you, and we will talk.'"

Jennifer had already given Hilary the lifeline she
needed when they spoke during the days between the
rape and pageant. This is what Hilary said: "My aunt
Jen offered to take me to coffee and be there for me. We
started meeting, and she'd ask how I was doing and be
there. She was instrumental in me deciding to continue to compete in the Miss Scottsdale Pageant. It
was four days later and I wasn't sure if I was up for it,
so I called Jen and asked for her advice. She told me
nobody would care either way—they'd love me even if
I didn't compete, and they would all be there to support me if I did. So I decided to compete. Later we continued meeting."

Jennifer lent a listening ear and encouraged Hilary
to journal her experiences and feelings. As her aunt
has mentored her, so Hilary shares her experience,
strength, and hope with others who have been through

similar life traumas. "I did a lot of journaling about what I was going through. We met once a week for about three hours each time and talked about how I was doing and what I was feeling.

"Sometimes we would focus on specific issues, whether it was fear, isolation, sadness, or anger, depending on what I was going through, what was in the forefront that week. And I know without a doubt that process and my meetings with Jen helped so much in my recovery because talking about what I went through is important. So many people just keep it bottled up inside.

"Being able to communicate what I was going through, instead of feeling isolated, helped so much. Being able to talk about it made me feel stronger, like I was doing something about it. I wasn't just taking it lying down. I was standing up and turning it into something positive.

"And my relationship with Jen has been a blessing because it was difficult at first to talk about it with my parents. That's not to say anything bad about my parents and my family; it's just difficult because they are so close to it and it affects them in a different way than it affected Jen. My parents were always there for me and ready and willing to talk. Jen has been awesome in the fact that I felt close enough to her to be able to open up to her but not too close where I worried about upsetting her and seeing tears."

Hilary found safe waters with Jen so she could be all whom God called her to be. Through their mentored friendship, they both wake up daily and live life with deeper meaning than before November 9. They both see how God meant them to be together for His purposes.

Joy and I have both reaped rich rewards. We talk about anything and everything for endless amounts of time. Time stands still when we are together. We send each other little thoughtful notes and gifts, sometimes big and beautiful, sometimes little and meaningful.

What you feed grows. We both fed and nurtured this outstanding and wonderful friendship. We both put good boundaries around our relationship—boundaries of mutual respect, confidentiality, trust, and understanding.

Like good counseling, mentoring doesn't tell you what to do. Rather, it offers the framework or principles which will bring about the best possible outcome. Mentoring's premise is wisdom, which when preceding action means everything will turn out OK. It gives me the confidence to believe it will be alright.

If I give you a fish when you're hungry, you will be filled for the day. If I teach you how to fish, you will eat for life. Joy taught me how to fish so I could eat for life. If she had always been telling me what to do, I'd only be able to eat for the day.

We've always had a lot of fun being together. Sometimes I wonder if she counts the number of times I've told the same story over again in the same way she does.

I was an open and willing questioner and listener, and Joy was a willing and available counselor and confidant. I don't think either one of us was conscious about it. It was just a natural consequence of our friendship.

The way Joy listened then and still listens now is a gift passed down to her from her mother. Joy learned from her mother that *listening feels like love*. Her mother listened to Joy and Joy knew it. If something became a burden in her heart, she knew she could tell her mother without any fear of judgment or condemnation.

Sometimes what we don't say speaks louder than what we do, and her mother had mastered the art of reading between the lines. Listening felt like love to Joy. Oftentimes perception is more important than reality. It has nothing to do with intelligence. Sometimes our loudest communication is simply the motives of our heart. What happened was not as important as how Joy felt.

"If you tell me about it," her mother would say to her, "no matter what it is, I will not punish you for telling the truth." Little Joy would confess. She loved talking with her mom, knowing that she was always heard. Listening is a gift that passed from Joy's mother to Joy to me. There's nothing like having children that brings out the real you. This came into sharp focus when my two daughters would talk with me.

Before I knew what Joy's mother had told her, I always told my children they would not get in trouble for telling the truth, so they've been good about being honest even when they didn't want to. However, there were times when I could sense the walls of my own agenda going up in my mind, which their communication couldn't climb.

My walls were put there by fear and taken down by Joy's love and my own 12-step recovery work. Our friendship was such a safe harbor, protected from the tempests of incivility and misunderstanding. *There is no fear in love [dread does not exist], but full-grown (complete, perfect) love turns fear out of doors and expels every trace of terror! For fear brings with it the thought of punishment, and [so] he who is afraid has not reached the full maturity of love [is not yet grown into love's complete perfection]. If anyone says, I love God, and hates (detests, abominates) his brother [in Christ], he is a liar; for he who does not love his brother, whom he has seen, cannot love God, Whom he has not seen* (1 Jo 4:18,20).

Growing pain and healing pain may hurt, but that

pain can be your doorway to healing. It was for me. You just have to be willing. . . . *uphold me with a willing spirit* (Ps 51:12).

I will never forget my friend Lisa who, after recuperating from corrective shoulder surgery, stopped taking narcotics to ease her intense discomfort. "I can handle the healing pain," she said. She did, and her shoulder works wonderfully. Lisa's words impacted my soul as she shared her strength with me. Just because pain hurts doesn't mean it's harmful. Just as Lisa handled her pain with so much dignity, so have I seen Joy do the same. In our friendship, I am learning to do likewise.

When you have a mentor or someone who is well into the journey of life, that person's wisdom and experience has the potential to catapult us to destiny because he or she has learned the hard lessons of life and is willing to pass them on to you. According to Joy's perspective, "Lots of people have gone through crushing things that they don't understand. We know God has a purpose for it—I don't know what the purpose is, but I know what mine was. I sometimes ask, 'God, why do I have to walk alone in this? Why can't somebody help me?' He explains to me, 'This is you and I walking together. Listen to My voice. They are learning to understand, and I'm giving you My compassion to touch them.' This sense is in me all the time, and it never goes away. It's not like something that was there and is gone. It is alive in my spirit constantly, and I thank God for it. There's a lesson learned and I am learning."

You are probably in a relationship with your mentor because you recognize you have a lot in common with each other. When you nurture this bond, your own personal growth and mutually met needs will be a natural result of your friendship.

You don't have to take notes on your lessons. *What*

you feed grows. When you communicate, stay in touch, and act on little things your friend says that you know are true, maturing will be a natural process.

Holding on to good relationships is harder than ever given a 63 percent divorce rate in the Christian church and so many broken, long-distance, and mobile relationships. The good news is that we can maintain strong, healthy connections with those we hold close to our hearts by simple nurturing. A little bit goes a long way.

When Joy's granddaughter Danni stopped by to change and refresh before her job, Joy put out her favorite fragrant bath gel next to a clean fluffy towel. It was a sweltering hot day in the Midwest, so Joy left a glass of cold water next to the bed waiting for her. *And whoever gives to one of these little ones [in rank or influence] even a cup of cold water because he is My disciple, surely I declare to you, he shall not lose his reward* (Ma 10:42).

Thoughtfulness works for my family, too. Making happy faces with the cantaloupe on my children's plates for lunch would prompt little smiles on their faces and in their hearts. Leaving a loving message on their voice mails keeps us connected now that they're older. Little things mean so much—even giving a smile when I don't feel like it.

We all want to be loved and feel like we belong. The need to have these essentials met in good and functional ways will have positive and long-lasting results. It is literally the difference between life and death. *Because you have been faithful and trustworthy in a very little [thing], you shall have authority over ten cities* (Lk 19:17). How we act toward people is a pretty good indication of how we feel about God.

A man's mind plans his way, but the Lord directs his steps and makes them sure (Pr 16:9). Joy wanted to be a psychiatrist. She reached the same end by a different means. Sometimes we want to be or do something because it is the closest thing we can imagine as being or describing our heart's desire. If we are in God's will, He will take us to our heart's desire and fulfill our calling so we make the mark. If it is not quite what God has in mind for us, He will bring us to our rightful place if we keep our rightful place in Him.

When asked recently if she feels a little "out of it" for not keeping up with computers and the exponential explosion of knowledge Joy replied, "I agree things are changing faster than in any other time of history and moving at a rate that is almost frightening. But changes in technology don't mean changes in human nature.

"With all the advantages also come more sorrows, problems, heartaches, loneliness, and disconnected families, fostering less and less bonding of human relationships, bringing confusion, crime, and despair. This is where we Christians come in. We have the answer through Jesus Christ—no, I do *not* feel out of it— I am excited about coming to the kingdom at such a time as this."

As Joy reflected on her years of counseling and the fruit of her ministry, she recalled, "How wonderful it is to sit together with another in counseling and feel the flow of the Holy Spirit opening, enlightening, recovering, and setting the captive free.

"To see the light shine throughout the saddened face and the whole countenance rejuvenated, and in the days, months, or years that follow the true destiny of that life being fulfilled." This is what Joy lives for.

You may have a general idea of where you're headed, but none of us knows exactly where we'll be a week from now, let alone one month, or even one year. If you could understand, the value of the process would be destroyed. What is important are the lessons you learn and the decisions you make today. *Today, if you would hear His voice and when you hear it, do not harden your hearts* (He 4:7). Jesus only gives us one day at a time; *so do not worry or be anxious about tomorrow, for tomorrow will have worries and anxieties of its own. Sufficient for each day is its own trouble* (Ma 6:34).

Joy makes learning fun. With her, I always feel great. I never walk away feeling worse. She makes it easy for me to learn.

Within the context of our companionship and throughout her life, Joy has demonstrated that success is the everyday gradual accomplishment of a worthwhile goal. Good news takes awhile to get around. Bad news travels fast. We don't hear about the good people the way we hear about the famous, notorious, or outstanding people. When we compare their outsides to our insides, we get into trouble. Then we either get disgusted, give up, and feel like a failure—unless we can be famous, we are made to feel that we have not achieved and will never be anything worthwhile. This addresses the psychological need to feel important but simply scratches the surface.

Hilary took her trauma and turned it into a triumph. She let go of her feelings of worthlessness and gave the glory to God for her healing and deep sense of worthiness and well-being.

"It's crazy . . . you know, this horrible thing happened, and He provided me with what I needed to get through. I'm doing so much better. You know, there are good days and there are bad days, and there are still hard things. But the difference is amazing from right after the rape. After it happened, I originally thought, 'OK, I need to change my platform, but I can't do it yet. I need to wait a little bit further in the recovery process.' After a couple of months of working with Jen and really thinking about it, I felt this passion that I needed to be out there making a difference right now to help other rape survivors. I was praying about it a lot and trying to decide if I should change my platform.

"At church one week, they were doing a message about Queen Esther, and the pastor read, *Who knows but that you have come to the kingdom for such a time as this and for this very occasion?* (Es 4:14). And I felt God telling me that now was the time to change the platform. Queen Esther was a wife to the king, which gave her the opportunity to save all those people. She had the choice to either accept that opportunity or ignore the call.

"It was like God was speaking directly to me saying, 'Look, this happened to you and you were blessed with the Miss Scottsdale title four days after. You have this incredible story that you can reach people with, so you should be out there doing it.' So I said, 'OK, God, You win, I'm going to do this.' " Hilary understands she isn't great because of what she's done. She is great because of her choices and the decisions she's made in the midst of incredible odds.

We need to go deeper to define our purpose. There is a difference between "great" and "famous." Sometimes someone can be both. Famous is external recognition for doing something outstanding. Many famous people are not great and often feel miserable inside. Famous may or may not be great. However, there are also great people who never become famous—happy, well-adjusted people who know they are living the life God designed for them. They are the great people. They don't strive for fame.

The important thing is to embrace your moments of destiny and experience their unfolding that leads to clarity, desire, and commitment to *your* personal fulfillment. Not a cheap imitation of someone else. You have all the God-given qualities within you for *true greatness*. Each of us has a *feeling of greatness* that can lead to true greatness. Joy used to think this was just in certain people, but her years of counseling taught her that every person has this buried inside. It only needs to be uncovered, awakened.

Do you want to go through all your life merely existing? You would not be reading this if you did. There is something crying out within you. This feeling is God's blessing to you that you may become all who He meant you to be. It is the "X" on the treasure map. Perhaps it may be weak at first, or hidden by circumstances and thoughts of discouragement.

Tommy Barnett, Joy's son, has pastored one of the largest churches in the nation for 23 years, and he recently celebrated his fiftieth year in ministry. Reflecting on the success of his ministry he said, "God doesn't call the qualified. He qualifies the called."

How does He do this? Jesus did not transform the men who were to become the spiritual fathers of the New Testament in one dramatic episode. Jesus mentored His disciples through friendship. When the student is ready, the teacher appears and we learn in recovery. When I am ready and willing, God's Word becomes *rhema*. Haven't you ever noticed you can read the same scripture a dozen times and one day it becomes *rhema*? It just jumps out at you and becomes alive in your soul. *Rhema* means "to become alive." *It is the Spirit Who gives life [He is the Life-giver]; the flesh conveys no benefit whatever [there is no profit in it]. The words (truths) that I have been speaking to you are spirit and life* (Jo 6:63). The Holy Spirit reveals God's Word to us in our mind and through our senses. He enables others to comfort, counsel, help, and strengthen us. I know when God has used someone to help me in answer to prayer. *But the Comforter (Counselor, Helper, Intercessor, Advocate, Strengthener, Standby), the Holy Spirit, Whom the Father will send in My name [in My place, to represent Me and act on My behalf], He will teach you all things. And He will cause you to recall (will remind you of, bring to your remembrance) everything I have told you* (Jo 14:26).

George was a well-known pastor, loved and respected in his community. God called George, qualifying him through Spirit-inspired revelation and insight. He felt he had friends who cared, and he even considered some as mentored friendships. Although he had what he thought was a strong support system, a growing depression was beginning to take its toll on his marriage, ministry, and family. When he turned to some of these friends, he felt let down.

"Men relate differently than women," reflected George. "I would not look at my life and see an individual that fit the role as a mentor, but there have been three or four men over the years who have been key in course correction. I sought for a year and even tried to find a way of starting or initiating some sort of a group of ministers where it was safe to be totally, gut-wrenchingly honest.

"Finding a group where I would be able to talk about fear or doubt or disbelief or anger at God, in a place that was safe enough but with men mature enough in faith and character not to react was important. The problem with most men, certainly anybody in the profession and in marriage, is when a man is asked a question he feels obligated to give an answer.

"Men learn the hard way that often when women ask a question they don't want an answer. They don't want to get fixed—they want somebody who will just listen, and vent.

"I have come into a group of four people who have the level of spiritual maturity. They all have gone through their own battles and walk with limps. It's safe enough to talk about things that are completely off-the-wall or straight theology, psychology, and science. I believe that I will see this season of my life as one of the most effective mentoring positions because it's just kind of an incredible experience.

"I was in the ministry from the time I was in junior high school, and there was never really a safe place. I needed a personal mentor then, and this may be one of the greatest tragedies for anybody in the professional life. To find that kind of peer connectedness would have filled such a great void.

"I had several people at the end of my public ministry who were struggling to survive. Many betrayed confidences, which was extremely hurtful and contributed to the ministry ending. Because I couldn't find the answers in myself, I couldn't find them in religious Christian counseling or any other of the standard mores. Since I was a senior pastor of a church, it was virtually impossible to find a peer group that I could trust. I hope that it is still not true."

George went through a terrible time losing his ministry and his marriage, and he struggled with depression. Depression so captured George's mind that he once mistook the effects of a medicine withdrawal as a depressive episode. "Depression to me is related to a feeling of being trapped where I don't have choices or feel the ability to make decisions."

He continued, "Now that I am keenly aware of this, I will not let myself get in those situations again because that really is what drove me out of the ministry and away from the direction I had been going in for 45 years. I felt absolutely trapped without choices. It was unbearable. I have no idea why I didn't kill myself. The hospitalization for my depression was just such a miraculous thing for me since I really did believe that I was mad at God and that God was mad at me."

God's Word was revealing *rhema* to George. *And you will know the Truth, and the Truth will set you free* (Jo 8:32).

"When I woke up to the reality that I was justified in my anger at myself and that I really had embraced a lot of lies, the fundamental truth remained, "the truth will set you free." Anytime I'm in bondage I realize it's because I believe a lie. If I'm free, it's because I'm embracing Truth.

"What triggered me was listening to a minister talk about timing and the saying which I have heard in 12-step recovery, "When the student's ready, the teacher will come." It is so true that when you're ready, the answer seems to come. The Holy Spirit is the Teacher in every case."

God prepared George to be ready to receive the Truth, His *rhema* for George. *I have still many things to say to you, but you are not able to bear them or to take them upon you or to grasp them now. But when He, the Spirit of Truth (the Truth-giving Spirit) comes, He will guide you into all the Truth (the whole, full Truth). For He will not speak His own message [on His own authority]; but He will tell whatever He hears [from the Father; He will give the message that has been given to Him], and He will announce and declare to you the things that are to come [that will happen in the future]* (Jo 16:12-13). The Living Word became real to George.

"When you hit somebody over the head with Bible information, you're not sharing the gospel. Forcing Bible facts and figures and verses is not sharing the Word." George reflected, "Maybe that sounds cynical, but it's got to be living that Word. It's got to be Life at the time of a person's need. We have been guilty of providing Bible bullets when someone needed a hand.

"And it's our God-awful need to be right and to think that we've got the answers to everybody's problems. It was not necessarily that many of the things Job's friends said were not accurate. Their words were right, but they were wrong."

George did not make this journey alone. "Sam has been a good friend for a very long time. Because he understood he was a fellow traveler on this road both religiously and in recovery, we had a bond. It was just him being there; he understood it; he had been there; this was not new territory; there was no judgment." Jesus qualified the call through mentoring. He mentored them through friendship.

For three years, He trudged with them down the dusty roads, over mountains, through valleys, in storm, in want, in every conceivable circumstance. They saw Him minister to all men—the lepers, the demon possessed, the harlots, the ecclesiastical dignitaries. They saw that He separated Himself from no one—the rich, the poor, the respected, the scorned—whatever their need. By His touch and His teaching, Jesus showed Himself to be the Answer. By His friendship and His love, Jesus showed Himself to be a wise, trusted, loyal Advisor.

In all He did and through their connection, He was conditioning the chosen 12. They had the most meaningful relationship imaginable. They were not just hobnobbing with the elite, but right out in the hard, realistic ruggedness of life, lived daily with Him. They were rubbing shoulders with all of humanity's woes. It was a real relationship, an authentic jewel. They were not social climbers. Their climb upward was walking with God and grasping hold of as many as possible, taking them with them.

Mentoring happens in families as well as in friendships. But just as not all friendships evolve into mentoring, not all family relationships evolve into mentoring.

Joy's husband Herschel was a pastor; for 44 years he led, nurtured, and encouraged his congregation. He loved people. He had his priorities ordered in integrity. Bringing out the best in people is a blessing both Joy and Hershel passed on to their children and grandchildren. These traits with which their offspring were born did *not* ensure the success of Herschel's descendents. Choosing to act upon these skills in a positive, functional, and beneficial way worked on their behalf. The blessing of bringing out the best in people was the result of mentoring because the baton was passed by choice.

As Joy and Herschel passed the baton, their children, Tommy and Vickie, took it and ran with it. Now the baton has passed on to all the grandchildren.

When raising my four children, I'll never forget asking Tommy before we moved from Phoenix, "How did all your kids not only come out OK, but be so outstanding?"

Tommy furrowed his brows as he always does when he's about to say something significant, then honestly and humbly replied, "I am not perfect. In fact, I made a lot of mistakes. But I loved them. Luke, Matthew, and Kristie all know that I love them."

To keep it simple, we'll start with Joy and Hershel, but this blessing probably extends way back and didn't originate necessarily with biological family. From Joy and Hershel, extending to Luke, Matthew, Kristie, and well beyond, I'm just one of the multitudes whose lives have been forever changed for the better as a result of their love.

Trust is one of the most significant ingredients in the friendship Joy and I share: trust. I trust in you. Trust, believe in, put my confidence in is another way of saying, "I have faith in you." The definition of faith is translated from the Greek word meaning "to leave it in the care of, lay it all on the line, even to death." Faith is not a struggle; it is a rest resulting from leaving all in our Heavenly Father's care!

A trusting child leans in confident repose upon the father's shoulder. We lean upon our God, rest, trust in repose upon Him.

Petra didn't always trust God. She was a self-proclaimed atheist from the time she was 16 until she was 35. She had reason to be. The day she ran away from home, her father knocked her into a bathtub where she cracked the back of her head open. He then pulled her out and held her against a wall by her throat until she passed out. When she came to, she quietly packed a tiny suitcase while her father stood over her telling her she was a whore and a tramp. She calmly walked out the front door.

Petra never said a word—not that she was leaving for good nor that she was running away. Nothing. He followed her about two miles in silence. That day she walked 18 miles. Her grandmother wouldn't take her in, and her boyfriend's parents would not help. So after spending a night next to a tree in a city park freezing, she walked all the way back home. Her father had locked all the doors which had never been locked before.

So Petra climbed through a window, got a tent, pillow, and blanket, then walked all the way back to town again. She did have $400 saved, so she spent the next six weeks living with her meager belongings. Yet God knew Petra, kept His eyes on her, and was with her even in the dark places. *He made darkness His secret hiding place . . .* (Ps 18:11). Her alcoholic parents never tried to look for her, even though she continued to attend high school. Later her mother told her they "couldn't find her." But she knew they never tried. When her boyfriend's parents found out she was pregnant, they let her live with them.

Petra was too afraid of drugs to deal or use them, but she thought about it. As a single parent, there were times they had nothing to eat and no working car. So she walked 12 miles round trip to work. During their lowest moments, Petra noticed an unusual pattern emerging. Some money would come in the mail. She found money blowing down the street. She even found money in the lake. God's *rhema* was working in Petra's life. Jesus said to Peter, *"Go down to the sea and throw in a hook. Take the first fish that comes up, and when you open its mouth you will find there a shekel. Take it and give it to them to pay the temple tax for Me and for yourself"* (Ma 17:27). Petra knew she was being taken care of by a Higher Power.

Petra's defining moment happened one night when she was driving very drunk. A state trooper pulled her over, took her license, saw she was in bad shape, and said he'd be right back. It was her breaking point and a pivotal point in time. Petra prayed the only way she knew how: "OK, God. You know I think you're bogus, and the only way I'm *ever* going to believe in You is if You get me out of this, I will believe in You. I can't say I'll go to church or go around blessing everyone all the time because to me that's just weird. But I will pray, I will change my life around, and I will believe in You."

What happened next was nothing short of a miracle. The state trooper returned to her car and told her there was an emergency down the road and he had to leave. His last words to Petra were, "Take the side street home and slow down."

As the state trooper walked away, he turned around, looked at Petra, winked and said, "God bless you." She cried like a baby all the way home. She had chosen God's way through her own brokenness and saw God with her. *When the righteous cry for help, the Lord hears, and delivers them out of all their distress and troubles. The Lord is close to those who are of a broken heart and saves such as are crushed with sorrow for sin and are humbly and thoroughly penitent* (Ps 34:17-18).

Petra now lives each day with greater purpose. She has forgiven her parents and lives to serve others in all she is and does. She lives God's greatness in her. She is learning to trust God.

When our trust is rooted in God, then we can trust others. *The fear of man brings a snare, but whoever leans on, trusts in, and puts his confidence in the Lord is safe and set on high* (Pr 29:25). This is the kind of trust Joy and I share. It takes work and it's worth it.

In our relationship, Joy showed me that goal and purpose are not the same. A goal is the place where a race is ended. Purpose is resolution or something one intends to get. Her goal was to become a psychiatrist. Her purpose was to help people. Whatever the goal is, it will always be based on purpose because purpose is the underlying reason for the goal.

Her goal changed when she married a pastor, but her purpose was the same. She still desired to help people, which she now did as a pastor's wife. In the end, she probably did more good.

Purpose and destiny are different, too. Destiny means a pre-determined course of events. Purpose implies intention. Joy and I were destined to meet, and we purpose to stay close always. Before we met, God had already planned how closely our lives would parallel. He prepared us to be able to work together effectively to accomplish His purpose for and through our lives. *Seek (aim at and strive after) first of all His kingdom and His righteousness (His way of doing and being right)* (Ma 6:33). This verse clearly states that Jesus must be first. Living for Him strengthens both goal and purpose. We must ask our Heavenly Father to give us the passion of intensity to *hold on* to this truth that gives meaning to all of life.

Our society is fast-paced and goal-oriented. While there is nothing inherently wrong with setting goals and reaching them, letting goals become a priority will disappoint you. Because goals are always changing, they were never meant to fill the vacuum in your soul. God created your spirit as a place for Him. As my trusted friend, Joy pushes me closer to Jesus, and I do likewise. We take great comfort in our relationship, but we knew before we met that it's all about God and not us. Maybe that is why it's so meaningful. Having goals and enjoying reaching them will be most rewarding when premised upon a purpose and destiny for living that are grounded in God's love. In our friendship, Joy loved me and showed me that Jesus *loves me.*

Billy Graham's daughter, Anne Graham Lotz, shares Joy's favorite thoughts on this. "Just give me Jesus. I think that's pretty much the answer," declared Joy. "Give me Jesus, and when we have Him in our hearts like you and I do, we constantly point one another in the right direction. That direction is toward Jesus, always."

I tell my children the two things I can count on in life are *change* and *God's love*. We handle change best when abiding in God's love. Joy showed me how to abide within the confines of our trusted friendship. After Hershel died, her sister died and Joy was only getting older. Her fear of becoming insignificant was becoming more real. She saw her life literally being passed on to me, and it made her life worth living.

Joy gives God the glory for this. "I became what you needed because God designed it. He designed all of the details and knew that He would be glorified and His purposes would be filled in our relationship together. And we understand that." When you clearly understand your purpose and destiny, you will choose goals based on this premise and have the most meaningful fulfillment. Mentoring through a trusted, loyal friend and advisor helps you get there.

This is really just a simple message that discourages depression and encourages everything good you've got going on in your life. We want you to learn to live life like a rag and squeeze every drop out of it.

There are wonderful relationships all around you just waiting to happen. You only need to show up and be willing. How can we show up when we feel so overwhelmed with endless, mundane daily activities and life in general?

Don, a spiritual and professional coach, travels worldwide for both corporations and ministry. He teaches five competencies effective when incorporated into your everyday life. They will work for you if you can identify them in your life. If you feel deficient in one of them, ask the Holy Spirit to give you a willingness to change. Regardless of the problems in your life, if you can identify the following, they will help you right where you are.

1. The Competency of Purpose: If you find purpose in everything you do, God can use you in that area. You have a unique ability to do

things that other people can't do just because you are driven by a need.

2. The Competency of Connection: No matter
what you're doing, no matter what's going
on, if you have connections in your life, you
will handle crisis better. You will manage
life's problems better.

3. The Competency of Perspective: If you have
the ability to measure and weigh things in
the right assessment of order and responsibility in your life, you will maintain balance
and your equilibrium. Let big things be big
and small be small.

4. The Competency of Learning: Learning is
the ability to gain understanding or skill in
your situation which will enable you to cope,
grow, and face one-on-one challenges.

5. The Competency of Change: If you have the
ability to experience transitions and adapt
to your different surroundings, then you will
find more energy to stay in the present and
enjoy the moment.

Personal Process Assessment

Joy mentored me through friendship. Friendships
happen in many settings and evolve in diverse ways,
but a precious few will grow into a mentoring relationship where you either become a loyal friend and advisor or the beneficiary of such a friend. How do you see
your friendships evolving? Which relationships in your
life have you received or given such love and guidance?
What are you doing currently to stay connected to
close confidants in your life?

Mentoring is counsel for the calling. It is not training, coaching, teaching, or parenting. Mentoring pro-

vides an essential spirituality necessary for overall growth and maturity. It involves spiritual impetus. Willingness is the contingency clause to defining your life's purpose and keeping it through mentoring. You define it when you're mentored. You hold on to it when you mentor. Mentoring is fun! Are you willing to do whatever it takes to see yourself succeed in your gifts and callings? As a mentor, do you make yourself available whenever the call comes? Do you accept the inconvenience of a phone call or interruption to stop what you are doing and accommodate the need?

- Destiny=Fate. Once you accept Jesus as your Savior and Lord, Heaven is your Destiny.
- Purpose=Intent. God wants you to wake up each morning with quiet resolve and determination in your heart to live this day to the fullest no matter what happens.
- Meaning=Message. God speaks to you through your circumstances every day. What is He saying to you?
- Goal=Target. It is the place where a project is finished or a trip is ended. Goals may change and have different meanings, but your purpose stays constant.

There is a difference between great and famous. Famous is an outside public recognition for accomplishment. Great is an inside understanding and recognition for who we are and living it out. God made us all great, not famous, but great. Through our trusted friendship, Joy showed me how to live great. Do you just want to be famous and fulfill a psychological need, or are you living out great the life God designed for you?

Don's Five Competencies are a simple, effective

way to cope with feeling overwhelmed and helping us stay in the present and enjoy each moment. They will work for you right now.

Speak to broken hearts and you speak to a large audience.

Charles Spurgeon

Man looks on the appearance, but God looks on the heart. Man considers the deeds, but God weighs the motives. To be always doing well and to think that you have done but little is the sign of the humble soul. To be unwilling to have any created being for our comfort is a sign of great purity and inward trust.

Thomas à Kempis

Be somebody to someone.

Mother Theresa

Iron sharpens iron; so a man sharpens the countenance of his friend [to show rage or worthy purpose]. Whoever tends the fig tree shall eat its fruit; so he who patiently and faithfully guards and heeds his master shall be honored. As in water face answers to and reflects face, so the heart of man to man.

Proverbs 27:17-19

Blessed be the God and Father of our Lord Jesus Christ, the Father of sympathy (pity and mercy) and the God [Who is the Source] of every comfort (consolation and encouragement), Who comforts (consoles and encourages) us in every trouble (calamity and affliction), so that we may also be able to comfort (console and encourage) those who are in any kind of trouble or distress, with the comfort (consolation and encouragement) with which we ourselves are comforted (consoled and encouraged) by God.

2 Corinthians 1:3-4

So then, as occasion and opportunity open up to us, let us do good [morally] to all people [not only being useful or profitable to them, but also doing what is for their spiritual good and advantage]. Be mindful to be a blessing, especially to those of the household of faith [those who belong to God's family with you, the believers].

Galatians 6:10

*Out in the highways and byways of life
Many are weary and sad.
Carry the sunshine where darkness is rife,
Making the sorrowing glad.
Chorus:
Make me a blessing
Make me a blessing
Out of my life may Jesus shine
Make me a blessing, oh Savior, I pray
Make me a blessing to someone today.*

Author Unknown

CHAPTER FOUR
Desire of Your Heart

*Delight yourself also in the Lord, and He will give you the desires
and secret petitions of your heart.*

Psalm 37:4

"It's lonely out on the limb, but that's where the fruit is."

Dr. Bill Bright (1921-2003)

*Bless (affectionately, gratefully praise) the Lord, O my soul;
and all that is [deepest] within me, bless His holy name!
Who satisfies your mouth [your necessity and desire at your
personal age and situation] with good so that your youth,
renewed, is like the eagle's [strong, overcoming, soaring]!*

Psalm 103:1,5

You have to want it. What is the desire of your heart? If you are dying of thirst, you will do anything to find that sip of water you know will save your life. This powerful motivator does more to impel us than our own natural gifts. It is why some people with seemingly little talent become so successful while others with great gifts go nowhere. The capabilities of some simply stand out and are quite obvious. It's like the world is theirs. And yet, they end up going nowhere.

Not talent. Not strength. Not ability. The secret is desire. You have to want it. What is the desire of your heart? What do you want? All people are born with individual gifts and talents.

There are other people who just seem to move along mundanely, yet do such dynamic deeds with their lives. Living with purpose has nothing to do with talent and everything to do with desire. What means the most to you?

"I get so frustrated over the decisions I see Kate making. She used to love the Lord so much. Now it seems like all she does is blame Him for all her problems," lamented Pamela about her friend. She had been good to Kate and was feeling rejected by her.

"I was really hoping to see her at my luncheon; she always seems to have the time to do what she wants. But when it comes to taking a little extra time for me, there's always an excuse. It's either her kids or she's too tired or there's something else going on. And I've done so much for her!"

"Pamela, you need to either talk to her or leave it at the cross and let go of it," I told her, "but you can't keep feeding it."

"Lindsey, do you know what I really believe?" Pamela baited me. "I really believe we do what we want to do."

Pamela hit the bull's eye. Both Pamela and Kate started on similar paths, loving Jesus with a life committed to Him, getting married, and having children. However, Kate started having problems in her marriage, resulting in divorce.

She said she didn't want divorce, but there seemed to be a pattern of wanting things her way, and often her actions were contrary to her words. Pamela felt badly because she believed that she wanted the relationship and Kate really didn't.

Misplaced desire is misspent desire. Because I learned an attitude of forgiveness from Joy, I learned how not to misplace my heart's desire, even though I often stumbled. I say this with a generous amount of reverential fear because I really believe taking the wrong turn is only one step away. So often in my 12-step recovery I have heard some of the most spiritually mature people I have ever known say, "It takes just the right mix of circumstance to bring me back down to Ground Zero."

Forgiveness is a process that includes feeling the pain of the offense, acknowledging it, and letting it go so that it loses its power over me. If I don't let go of the anger I have toward someone, I am giving my power to them. Joy gave me permission to have my feelings. They are what enabled me to learn to complete the process and then let go. I cease to feel resentment against the person; I forgive the person, not the evil.

Each of us has our own program of forgiveness. Don already knew how to forgive, knew what he wanted, and had plenty of reason to forgive. "If you had asked me to talk about anything in the process I've gone through in the last six years, I probably wouldn't say that forgiveness is an issue. I cannot remember when I didn't forgive.

"I cannot say to you that I had a moment when I realized I was unforgiving and I needed to forgive. I had to apply the principle daily, but I don't think I ever came to the point where I thought my life was out of control because I couldn't forgive these people and events.

"I had moments of extreme hurt, pain, and isolation. I was in Australia in 1999 teaching at some conferences. I'd been there for five or six weeks. After 16 or 17 years spent speaking in Australia, I had pretty much become accustomed to driving on the other side of the road. I had borrowed a car from a very good pastor friend of mine, and when I came over a hill in Melbourne, I had a horrible accident.

"All I remember about the wreck is hitting a semi-truck, and then when I came to I was prostrate on the very top of the car. I had obviously gotten out of the car and climbed on the roof. A truck driver woke me up saying, 'Mate, are you OK?'

"'Yes, I think so.' There were some glass cuts, but that was about it; however, the car was totaled—a brand new car.

"'How did I get on top of the car?'

"'You were lying on top of this car praying for God to heal the car because it belonged to your best friend.' A few minutes later, I sat in the car filling out a police report, then I actually drove to the Chinese Coalition of Believers in Australia. Within two hours of the accident, I taught at a very large conference.

"Through that accident, the Lord told me my life was going to crash, but I would be spared. My mind flashed back to my prostrate form praying on top of the car when the truck driver said, 'The car's not gonna make it, Mate, but you're gonna make it.' That was the Word of the Lord to me.

"The words of this crazy Australian truck driver, whom I don't know and haven't met since, rang clear. 'The car's not gonna make it, but you are.' I remembered those words returning from Australia. Within a few months, my wife moved out, I resigned my ministry, and my son was in the hospital with multiple surgeries. I spent the holidays in ICU with my son, who was very ill.

"He went into a rehab home for quite a while, but he eventually died. During this time, a moment of healing and forgiveness occurred. After the divorce, my wife and her fiancé (the man she became involved with) asked forgiveness of my older son and me. We forgave them, so there were moments of forgiveness during that time.

"I had been in ministry almost 25 years, but during the six months in the hospital only one pastor visited me. After my son's death, I confronted my friends with my feelings of abandonment. They shared some things with me that they wished I had done better. Again, there were moments of forgiveness and sharing. We spent the better part of a day together talking.

"My burden has always been for leaders. I had been in the work of restoring leaders and now, for the first time in my life, I was in the outer circle instead of the mainstream. They were looking for me to do what I had always done because they didn't grasp the challenges of my son's illnesses. I was fighting for the life of my son.

"The nature of ministry is a convoluted domino effect. When one thing falls, everything falls. In most careers, you can have a marriage problem, and it doesn't mean you have to lose your job. Ministry is different. Whether it's your fault, whether it's their fault, no matter who is to blame, the minister is responsible.

"I wanted distance from my problems. So I resigned all senior leadership positions that had any kind of ministry responsibility. I was hoping my wife and I would experience a time of healing, but that didn't happen. Also, I didn't want to poison any of those churches with my marital difficulties. The marriage challenges of pastors tend to infect a congregation, so the best thing I could do was step aside. I worked years starting ministries, and I didn't want them suffer because my wife and I were separating.

"We needed to get out of the mainstream of things, but I had hoped the people who loved us would find us. Between the ministry, my son, and my wife, one thing kept me going—forgiveness.

"I took ownership of things. I had failed in my own responsibilities. I always found enough stuff for me to deal with that I didn't focus on other people's failures,

but I did confront them. I'd give people a chance to respond so I didn't hide in a corner and get mad.

"When I started to pout, I had one or two good
friends who would hold on to me and help me face
those issues. They had been through the fire, too. At
the end of a long day, a lot of the things that would
burn off my life were like the ropes of Shadrach, Meshach, and Abednego."

In Daniel 3, these three men refused to worship the
king Nebuchadnezzar and worshiped God only. Nebuchadnezzar threw them into a fiery furnace, but God
protected them and they emerged from the furnace un-
scathed. *These men—that the fire had no power upon
their bodies, nor was the hair of their head singed; neither were their garments scorched or changed in color
or condition, nor had even the smell of smoke clung to
them. Then Nebuchadnezzar said, Blessed be the God
of Shadrach, Meshach, and Abednego, Who has sent
His angel and delivered His servants who believed in,
trusted in, and relied on Him! And they set aside the
king's command and yielded their bodies rather than
serve or worship any god except their own God* (Da
3:27-28).

Don continued, "Because the life of God's kingdom
is within you wherever you are, it naturally will over-
flow. So when we find ourselves in the public sector
and ministry opportunities avail themselves, we can
embrace opportunities to disciple.

"I have become very comfortable without the title
of Evangelist or Pastor. I still enjoy a successful ministry as a servant in the workplace watching God work
in people's lives. However, I felt bitter about having my
very good reputation taken away. I felt the one thing I
did not want to lose was my reputation. Having faced
the fear of loss and the reality of losing it, I don't know

what I was guarding because those things we hold so dear are usually holding us back from accomplishing what God would do.

"I probably don't have a reputation now. Once I divorced, there are certain groups of people where I will never be 'one of the boys' again. Divorce is a brand, but it has not stopped the kingdom of God, and I feel more fulfilled today than ever before."

Don truly experienced a Job-like trauma. He lost his wife, his livelihood, his son, and his reputation. But what he wanted more than anything was God, and God knew this. He continued to delight himself in the Lord, take matters straight to the heart of God, and work through the pain with God Himself.

"It was how I responded to those tough places and tough times that became my calling card of ministry. I've preached probably a thousand sermons, but I don't know that I've lived in the kingdom more than I have in my last five years. I lost everything. For me, not only has forgiveness not been a life issue on this stuff, it's just gratefulness. What's paramount is I find things to be grateful for.

"There were times I was clearly mad—I was mad at God for setting up things the way He did. I said that I should be able to lose *this* without losing all *that*! But I was very honest with Him about it.

Slowly the ashes of Don's life became the fertile soil for new growth. Don started his own coaching and consulting company. He still travels worldwide conducting corporate seminars for personal growth and career development. He still has a heart for pastors, and he works with them incognito. He is remarried and works closely with his son.

Over the years, Joy's forgiveness took root in my soul, but it was about to be tested to its limit. God created our spirits like a vacuum that was meant to be filled with Him and by Him. He vividly showed me this in the most extraordinary way.

Swimming is my favorite sport because it is quiet, invigorating, and I can pray and enjoy the solitude. I have cognizance that I am dependent upon Jesus for every breath that I take.

One day, praying deeply and fervently, I purposefully swam my laps. Overhead, the soft white fluffy clouds lazily drifting across the sunny sky belied the turbulent storm in my mind. My life was full with my family, engaging activities, and meaningful relationships. However, when fulfillment turned into complacency, I started feeling restless.

Michael was working long hours as always, which will sometimes trigger my fear of abandonment. I was feeling abandoned and angry about it, but instead of taking the matter straight to the heart of God, I started feeding my resentment and self-pity. "I am always alone running our household! I feel more like a single mom than a married one!" The clouds of darkness usually gather gradually, setting in as we transgress the boundaries in our mind. The battle is won or lost in the mind.

As I swam and waged war with powerful and seductive thoughts, emotions, and spirits, I finally reached the end of my rope, praying in a spirit of helplessness, submission, and repentance, fighting, then searching for the meaning of my tempestuous thoughts and emotions. In the vortex of my spiritual storm, I had a vision of a huge dark hole in my spirit. It was a vast void, and I was trying to fill it with something that wasn't meant to be there. Feeding my wandering mind was nothing more than an attempt to fill my soul in a way that only God can fill it. This was my defining moment. "Oh, God," I prayed, "Fill this space in my spirit with You, and in Jesus' name, set me free!"

I will never forget that feeling of being unshackled. Making such a good choice was a direct result of my relationship with Joy and what I learned from her. Those plaguing thoughts vanished, and a sense of peace and well being were as quickly restored as the storm had brewed.

My longing wasn't actually for a better situation, more clothes, or another donut. My misplaced desire was in essence a deep need for God to fill my spirit. Eating, spending, drugs, alcohol, sex, shopping, sports activities, even church activities may be motivated by an attempt to fill a void that only God can complete. Had I acted on it, my misplaced desire would have become misspent. What I truly want more than anything else is God's Will over my way.

And I believe what He wants for me are loving, healthy relationships with my husband, family, and friends regardless of any accompanying storms. But if that's what I really want, I must work for it. But what I always need is Jesus to fill the void regardless of my want. The beautiful mystery and meaning of it all is that when I am back abiding in the Vine, my need becomes my want and I am satisfied.

Zach had it all. Tall, dark, and handsome, he was a successful doctor with a beautiful girlfriend, plenty of friends, fast cars, and a taste for adventure. He loved the Lord, went to church once in a while, and kept a Bible near his bed. In 1996, he felt a funny feeling in his chest—like his heart was skipping beats. Then it passed.

Less than a year later in the fall of 1997, Zach woke up at 2:00 a.m., his bed soaked with sweat, his heart racing at almost 200 beats per minute. He could no longer deny what lay before him. The diagnosis came back as lone arterial fibrillation, a very rare and untreatable heart condition.

"At that time," said Zach, "There was essentially no cure for the disease. I was absolutely healthy otherwise. Some people with this disease will have an episode once to twice a year, but it was happening to me multiple times during the week. It was completely debilitating and sent me into a significant depression.

"Many types of medications were used to try to control it—none of which worked effectively. Not only that, the medications caused me to lose 15 pounds, and I was not overweight. I went from having one of the busiest medical practices to not working at all.

"I discovered this was unlike some other irregular heartbeats that could be treated. The research into curative intervention was only in its infancy. So my options were very limited, and all I could do was hope for a cure because nothing else was able to address it.

"I don't know what I would have done without my brother, Andrew. He was the one I was close to at the time, even more so than my girlfriend. He was my spiritual coach. I mean, he was there for everything. Because we were close, he could empathize in terms of my battles with the disease. It was a disease that very few people understood at that time, even the cardiologists.

"Andrew knew how I felt; my being a doctor and understanding it all made me feel even more helpless and hopeless. He was a priceless support and encouragement in my deep despair. It definitely brought me to my knees. I went from having everything to having nothing. Nothing else mattered. It was an overwhelmingly oppressive disease process, especially for someone who otherwise was healthy.

"It always helps to have another human there. Andrew was the lifeline God used to bring me to Him. Ultimately, all the power comes from above, but I think God sends us individuals who are compatible with us, somebody who can really understand our fears and our circumstances. This was a point where I could have cursed God, but I sought God instead. He pruned away any worldly enticements since none of that mattered anymore.

"It didn't matter that I had Ferraris, homes, attractive women, a bustling medical practice, a good physique, and the ability to do whatever I wanted. None of that was accessible to me anymore, but I didn't care because my health was gone. Although I never attempted suicide, there were certainly times when I wished I could die.

"I knew Jesus as my Savior, and my relationship with God was one of acceptance and acknowledgement of His existence, though not a spiritually integrated existence with Him. Fortunately, I made the right choice at that time and I said, 'Just give me a Bible and all I'm going to do is sit down and read this Bible. I'm going to understand what the story of Calvary is all about, what the resurrection of Jesus means to me, and what the essence of all this is.'

"For the first time in my life, I pulled out the Bible and started reading the New Testament from the very beginning. I was not working, and every day was a struggle getting out of bed, dealing with the meds and hoping my heartbeat would be in the correct fashion that day. I would simply read and study Scripture from an objective and historical perspective rather than from any ethereal or mythological perspective. I dove in and started digging, and there was a real purity that I found to the message.

"There was no longer anything about my own perspective, a Catholic perspective, any other religious

perspective—it was simply the objective historical perspective. The more I studied it, the more real it became. Sometimes you may hear someone speak about
a spiritual epiphany or some kind of spiritual event
that changed their lives. *And it shall come to pass in*
the last days, God declares, that I will pour out of My
Spirit upon all mankind, and your sons and your
daughters shall prophesy [telling forth the divine coun-
sels] and your young men shall see visions (divinely
granted appearances), and your old men shall dream
[divinely suggested] dreams (Ac 2:17).

"I had experiences and revelations during my journey through intense biblical study that were objective,
physical miracles that could never be explained empir-
ically by any scientific method. These were things I experienced that could not be explained any other way
than by something beyond this world."

> *True, there is nothing to be gained by it, but [as*
> *I am obliged] to boast, I will go on to visions and*
> *revelations of the Lord. I know a man in Christ*
> *who fourteen years ago—whether in the body or*
> *out of the body I do not know, God knows—was*
> *caught up to the third heaven. And I know that*
> *this man—whether in the body or away from the*
> *body I do not know, God knows—was caught up*
> *into paradise, and he heard utterances beyond*
> *the power of man to put into words, which man*
> *is not permitted to utter. Of this same [man's ex-*
> *periences] I will boast, but of myself (personally)*
> *I will not boast, except as regards my infirmities*
> *(my weaknesses).*
>
> 2 Corinthians 12:1-5

God continued showing Himself to Zach, becoming
the desire of his heart; this desire was not misspent.

Zach chose to meet God in his darkest hour, not to blame Him for taking everything away. It looked like death was inevitable. Zach was ready, but God wasn't ready for Zach.

"God spoke to me through His Word, and it began to give me hope. I was being tested, still fighting the arrhythmia. One night I was in bed, experiencing the arrhythmia and at the end of my rope, even after believing God was speaking to me through His Word.

"I had a dream, but people would say, 'You had this dream in a state between wakefulness and sleepiness.' They did not believe God spoke to me directly through a dream. But I know that what happened that night was as real as the sun rising. God told me that by His name I would be healed. I started working at a slow pace and no longer spent nights in the hospital. Whenever I would hear of cardiologists or physiologists who had any experience in curing my heart disease, I would get on a plane and meet them. Finally, God led me to a cardiologist in Provo, Utah who could burn the spot on my heart that was causing the irregular heartbeat.

"A spiritual journey means making spiritual friends; I had fellow believers praying for me, and I knew God was going to hear their prayers for this experimental procedure. I thought of how vehemently Jesus prayed in the Garden of Gethsemane, and the thought gave me trust in the power of prayer. I think He prayed aggressively all the time.

"The surgery was successful, but it took time to heal. After the operation, on the flight home, I felt the irregular heartbeat. Once again, I was acutely discouraged and depressed, but it didn't stop my prayers or my hope because I resolved to have the surgery again when the technology improved. Instead, the irregularities in my heartbeat reduced, and I weaned myself off the medications. Since my surgery, five years have passed, I have not had any reoccurrences, and I'm off all medications.

"I work at a less intense level, but I still do very well; I'm married and have an eight-month-old daughter who is the newest miracle in my life. I can look back on what I went through, knowing I love God more than I ever have. I have seen how Christ works. He prepared me for a new way of living and a new way of serving others."

God used Zach's brother Andrew (who knew Jesus) to push Zach in Jesus' direction. Because Zach has learned how to hear from God, he listens when he feels God is speaking about the circumstances in his life. Instead of another home for himself, he bought a home that is now used as a halfway house for recovering drug addicts and alcoholics, helping them transition into a normal way of living with Jesus' help.

"I give back and serve as best I can simply because I love God, Jesus, and the Holy Spirit as much as I do."

In Brother Lawrence's book, *The Practice of the Presence of God*, he reflects, "What should we set as the ultimate goal in this life? The answer: The most perfect worshipers of God we can possibly be, like we hope for ourselves throughout eternity."

Ever since Joy can remember, she just loved and worshipped God as did her mother. She reflected, "I had no one to talk to about the things my stepfather had done to me. We didn't talk about private affairs outside the family. But my mother couldn't help me—she didn't know how to help me. I learned this in many areas of my life: that God really is my only Source, and as I look to Him, I learn to hear His voice—I hear it inside of me, in my spirit. It is confirmed by my spirit, and I know this is God. It may not always be the way that is easiest for me to go, but it is the way I must go in order to fulfill God's purpose in my life.

"I never resented my mother's situation. God, I know, helped me to understand her situation because we were both part of a situation that neither one of us could do anything about. I know a lot of children resent their mothers, but I never did. My mother and I always had a wonderful understanding about things.

"After my daddy died, I learned to read my mother's expressions and understand her heart. I knew there were some things she had no control over, and I knew her heart was with me. When I was 15, she took me to Bible college to leave me there, but I didn't want to stay. My mother understood my cry, and she was not angry or mean with me. I felt such compassion in her because she was in the same bondage I was in, and there was not one thing we could do. We had to look to God."

The absence of love and belonging created inside Joy a craving to heal the hurt in other people. She wanted to give to others what she knew she needed. Born into a family that loved Jesus, she treasured the memory of the unconditional love lavished by her parents when she was small. Although she was gifted with wonderful people skills, Joy ended up living a life serving others because she *wanted* to.

Joy's motivation to this day is *desire*. The only contingency clause is "willingness." God never ignores our freedom of choice, although He does encourage us to make choices that bring life by putting it before us.

Joy is still a much sought after speaker in greater Kansas City. A recent speaking engagement found her before a Christian conference of teens. She is a favorite counselor among young singles and the newly married. She's not an old person—she meets you where you're at, and she loves what she does.

One of the greatest frustrations is knowing what

we want but not how to get there. Joy mentored me in forgiveness. The path to having my desire fulfilled was forgiveness and letting go. Whatever your issues are or the lessons are that need to be faced, God will provide for you when you call out to Him.

Wherever you harbor unresolved conflict or malice, you will find yourself a victim. You also may become the perpetrator of the very thing you hate. Forgiveness is a process that often takes years to work through. So the sooner forgiveness became an attitude, the faster the victim is set free. Forgiveness is so vital because it is God's nature to forgive. He made us in His likeness, so this is what will fit us best. Forgiveness has been a process for both of us and a blessing passed down to me from Joy. It was the key to keeping me from further temptation. I wanted it and I was ready for it. I had major issues of reproach that I had to relinquish. Reproach was taking its toll on me spiritually, mentally, and physically. There were just too many liabilities that came with it. If temptation is the road to misspent desire, then forgiveness was the turn that put me back on track. I had to be willing to be honest with myself.

Forgiveness is only one of many lessons I learned through Joy's life. In her story, with all her heart, Joy truly wanted to poison her cruel stepfather. But instead of marching off to the medicine cabinet, she went into her bedroom and with outstretched arms cried, "Oh, God, please help me. Help me! Give me an understanding heart so I can help other people, so they won't have to hurt like I do." That defining moment surged new strength into Joy's heart. She knew it was a decision coupled with a strong emotion and intent. She knew what she was going to do. This astounding moment of impact had determined her destiny. Joy responded the way she did because the love she had in her heart was greater than the hate around her.

Joy taught me that having hatred and horrible feelings about an offender and an offense is valid and necessary to acknowledge. It is part of the process of forgiveness. However, if hatred is my weapon of defense or I feel it's the only power I possess in the situation, then I stop short of fulfilling my purpose. I took the baton as she passed it to me and chose to work through the pain of forgiveness. This incredible process became an attitude first for Joy, then for me, and it will for you.

How do you achieve this? How can you have such a connected relationship, grow and live with such a good feeling and sense of well-being? Joy and I have found some essential elements that contributed to the extraordinary wealth of our friendship. Good friendships don't just happen. They are built. The better the principles used, the better the relationship will be.

Joy's mentoring showed me how to live. You can live your whole life and still not know how to live. Mattie Stepanek died of muscular dystrophy at age 13. Yet he probably lived a life fuller than most may ever see. He lived life because he knew he was dying. He wanted to experience life, and his mom helped him live it.

Although I have no power over the day of my death, I think I'll live a long time like Joy, who is 86 and has a personal trainer. She gets breathless from working out—not from a heart that doesn't work. The following are tips to mentoring which worked for us and will help you get there.

1. Discover Your Heart's Desire

What means more to you than anything else in the entire world? What gets your heart beating, your mind racing with more possibilities than you can possibly imagine? You must define what you want and decide it's what you really want.

Paint a picture in your mind. Hold on to it as if your life depends on it. In reality, the quality of your life may actually depend on your dream. Once you've defined the desire of your heart, you can live for it. Pray and ask God to reveal to you by His Holy Spirit what really means the most to you. Sometimes what I think I want isn't really what I want. Like oil and vinegar, once it settles, the oil always rises to the top. Let His Holy Spirit settle you and let your desires surface.

I live for Jesus. He is my heart's desire. He gave me a beautiful husband, a loving family, and the gift of encouragement. God brought Joy into my life to help me see my heart's desire fulfilled by bringing me to a higher level of spiritual maturity and emotional fulfillment that equipped me for my role as a person and as a woman.

When we met, Joy was already a widow, but her husband was a leader as my husband is a leader. Early on, I saw my need to be a strong wife and sensed my own immaturity even if I didn't verbalize it. She was a leader's wife. She had what I needed, and God knew this. I didn't pray for a mentor that would teach me how to be a leader's wife, but I did pray for God's will to be done in my life so I could be all who He meant me to be. She was the tool of God's will.

Now that I am acquiring my own 20/20 hindsight, I realize how immature I was when Joy and I first met, and how she must have been pleased at any progress I made.

2. Cultivate a Good Friendship

The root of every meaningful mentoring relationship is friendship. A friendship never starts in drudgery, but rather with a fun, intriguing interest about each other that drives the camaraderie. You will usually find that you share common interests. You just hit it off with each other.

As you gain history with each other, trust develops the atmosphere that a confidante needs. Because fun is part of a good friendship, learning becomes easy when life's lessons are taught this way.

Using good principles of civility, we esteemed and promoted each other. We would rather be bridge builders than burners. I knew what I wanted when I met Joy, and her friendship and mentoring helped me to hold on to what I already wanted. My dream is the same, but I am a little older and a little wiser.

3. Find the Right Fit

Not every friendship evolves into a mentoring relationship. My friendships happen in many different settings. Some are in church, some are in school activities, some are moms of my children's friends, and others are at my husband's work. Each friendship has its own traits and evolves in different ways, including mentoring.

In mentoring, whether you are teaching or learning, if it doesn't fit, it never will, so don't wear it. You have to be able to communicate in every way. I have two exquisite dresses Michael had tailored for me in Hong Kong. Those dresses fit like a glove.

When Alexandra met Francesca, they immediately connected. Whether you call it "chemistry" or intuition, it is still Holy Spirit-inspired and God-ordained. God made us, and He knows who is going to fit with us.

Hilary tried other counselors. They didn't work, but her Aunt Jen did. They both felt God meant them to be together.

If you are trying to make it fit, it probably isn't meant to be. Joy and I have personalities that fit each other perfectly. It's almost like we know what we're thinking before we say it. And we can always pick up where we left off. We know how we work.

4. Complement—Don't Compete With—Each Other

Our age difference definitely complements us. We find no competition or insecurity in each other's company.

We prioritize the important even if it is something little, but we let go of petty trivia even when it's big. We work with each other and for each other, not ever against each other or with poor motives. Poor motives would be anything rooted in self-centeredness.

Joy understands that I want what she has, not for the sake of taking it from her, but to make myself a better person and the world around me a better place. When I gain ground in my learning curve, Joy finds great satisfaction because she knows her life's lessons have been made worthwhile. It's all about God and His purpose for our lives together, and we find deep spiritual fulfillment in living this life drawn by His calling.

5. Set Good Ground Rules

I don't call Joy before 10 a.m. She is not a morning person. Actually, neither am I. I have to get up at 6 a.m. if the kids are going to be on time for school, so I don't call her early. She knows I'll let voice mail pick up during dinner and homework, so she waits until the children are in bed before calling.

Out of understanding the need for healthy boundaries, we work around each other's needs, likes, and dislikes. I mind my manners with Joy and treat her with a lot of respect and deference. She has earned it and deserves it. *Let him who receives instruction in the Word [of God] share all good things with his teacher [contributing to his support]* (Ga 6:6). She is cognizant and appreciative of my unspoken effort.

6. Speak the Truth in Love

Because I am forthright, sometimes my spicy words need to be tamed with diplomacy. There's nothing wrong with being straightforward and honest, but pepper it with being blunt and caustic, and you will find communications stops.

Joy mentored me in speaking the truth in love. Although Joy doesn't mind my approach because she doesn't take offense, she understands how I think. It is difficult to offend Joy and it is difficult to offend me.

We are so civil with each other. In M. Scott Peck's *A World Waiting to Be Born: Civility Rediscovered*, he defines civility as "consciously motivated organizational behavior that is ethical in submission to a Higher Power." He also says thoughtfulness takes time. I've seen this in Joy and am integrating this characteristic of thoughtfulness that belies civility in how I think, and it certainly shows in our relationship.

I have learned emotional hurt is often a choice. We work through differences easily and without ruffling our feathers. Maybe that's why misunderstanding rarely happens between us.

We don't talk about other people and what's going on with them. We just deal with ourselves and things as they relate to us. I don't have time to be taking other people's inventory. My own list is long enough and that's all I have time for. Gossip also tends to deflate friendships.

There is a difference between keeping secrets [*It is the glory of God to conceal a thing* (Pr 25:2)] and keeping confidence [*Argue your cause with your neighbor himself; discover not and disclose not another's secret, lest he who hears you revile you and bring shame upon you and your ill repute have no end* (Pr 25:9-10)]. As a leader's wife, I've seen and heard so much over the years that I instinctively knew what had to be kept confidential. Joy confirmed this through her own attitudes and actions.

7. Find a Need and Fill It

Seeing the need lays the groundwork for mentoring. God made our human nature to meet our needs whenever they occur. Whether we are conscious of them or not, we're looking to meet that need.

When I met Joy, I was attracted to her personality. As our friendship grew, I unconsciously recognized something in her that I needed or wanted. She had a life of wisdom and love. It was what I wanted, and she was willing to share her life with me.

Joy's spiritual experience and wisdom caused the most phenomenal growth in me as I integrated those same principles in my life. I needed her and she needed me. Jesus said it is the sick who need the doctor. If you don't acknowledge the need, you won't get the need met. In my 12-step recovery program, service and sponsorship find and fill the need. I mature faster with a sponsor. I stay grounded in my growth as a sponsor. Service gives me the chance to fill someone else's needs and have my needs filled at the same time.

One of mentoring's most outstanding qualities is spiritual impetus coupled with encouragement. Look at how our country grieved the death of President

Ronald Reagan. His chaplain made the most remarkable comment about how the Holy Spirit was "deeply imbedded in the spiritual DNA of Ronald Reagan." This president left a lasting legacy of hope and encouragement.

8. Experience Mutual and Unconditional Love

The love that Joy and I have for each other is a reasonable, intentional, spiritual devotion that is inspired by God's love for us. It is a committed love based on an act of each of our wills.

We believe the best in each other; we are patient and kind with each other. "You can do no wrong in my eyes," I sometimes tease her when she mentions a personal weakness that seems major to her but minor to me.

I have always had a deep desire for truth in my life. This desire in college spurned my quest for God. He showed me the Truth in Jesus. So when I met Joy, I perceived immediately she had a level of honesty that I appreciated and wanted in my own life.

We don't insist on our way, and we pay little attention to our differences. We acknowledge our distinctions, but don't focus on them. I really feel that in the beginning of our friendship, Joy believed better in me than I did in myself. She showed me so much unconditional undeniable love. This has meant more to me than anything because this is what I am learning to pass on to my family and friends.

St. Francis of Assisi proclaimed that we go and preach the Gospel and use words if we have to. God uses people to express His love, and He used Joy to tell me how much He loves me. She never said, "Jesus loves you, Lindsey." She lives His love in what she is and what she still does.

9. Hold on by Letting Go

You have to hold on with all your heart because there will be so many sidetracks and pitfalls in the road that it may be impossible to hold on to your desire or dream. This paradox is a foundational spiritual principle that simply means to surrender.

When things don't seem to be working as I wanted them to, I need to leave my dream and desire with God and trust Him for the results. Sometimes the ambition has to die before it comes to life. If I try to work it out my way, then I may prevent my heart's desire from happening simply because my way was in the way.

Zach had it all, but when he lost his health he could enjoy nothing. He was a doctor tormented by the knowledge there was no known cure for his heart disease. It took a toxic level of medication to treat his symptoms so he lost either way. In his darkest moment, he heard God speak. He had to let go in the midst of excruciating physical pain and imminent death. In the center of his deepest fear, he let go of all his expectations and learned in the process to hold on to Jesus.

Joy's encouragement in those moments of deepest, darkest discouragement helped me stay the course. Often it wasn't anything she said or did; just her listening and being there validated what I was going through and made it all worthwhile in that moment. She gave me reason to keep going.

I held on to what I wanted through mentoring. Joy taught me how to let go. If she could do it, so could I. I held on by letting go.

10. Let Him Do What You Can't

Sometimes I hold on to something so tightly my knuckles are white. I am too afraid to let go. The verse, *and He Himself existed before all things, and in Him all things consist (cohere, are held together)* (Col 1:17), has enabled me to loosen my grip on my way. Even when I've done all I can, there will still be times when I feel like I've hit a roadblock in my relationship or my efforts aren't enough. Painting a picture of Jesus holding everything together helps me to let Him handle my problem.

I really believe I walk this life alone with Jesus. Joy won't be standing there with me on Judgment Day. I will stand alone with Jesus. This means only I can take responsibility for my own attitudes and actions. However, I'll see her just beyond the cross, waving at me and waiting for me so we can catch up!

The first three steps in my recovery program say, "I can't. God can. I think I'll let Him." God gives; God takes away. It's all about Him, not me. The essence of my walk with Jesus and His keeping me in a recovery mode is learning that life revolves around Him and not me.

Naomi and Ruth perfectly personify these ten mentoring tips in the Book of Ruth. Living in a land of famine, Ruth's desire was to follow God.

In the days when the judges ruled, there was a famine in the land. And a certain man of Bethlehem of Judah went to sojourn in the country of Moab, he, his wife, and his two sons. That man's name was Elimelech and his wife's name was Naomi and his two sons were named Mahlon [invalid] and Chilion [pining]; they were Ephrathites from Bethlehem of Judah. They went to the country of Moab and continued there. But Elimelech, who was Naomi's husband, died, and she was left with her two sons. And they took wives from the women of Moab;

*the name of the one was Orpah and the name of
the other Ruth. They dwelt there about ten years;
And Mahlon and Chilion died also, both of
them, so the woman was bereft of the two sons
and her husband. Then she arose with her
daughters-in-law to return from the country of
Moab, for she had heard in Moab how the Lord
had visited His people in giving them food*

Ruth 1:1-6

As hungry as she was, given the choice between
staying in her own homeland, this woman would prefer to become a stranger in a foreign land in her search
for food. Ruth would rather die than be without the
God she saw in Naomi. *"Where you die I will die and
there will I be buried. The Lord do so to me, and more
also, if anything but death parts me from you"* (Ru
1:17). For the bread God was ultimately calling them
to was the Bread of Life. Ruth would become the great-
grandmother of David, the lineage of Jesus.

They had the hallmark of a strong friendship. On
the same side in a struggle for survival from starva-
tion, they supported and sympathized with each other.
Naomi told Ruth, *"May the Lord deal kindly with you
as you have dealt with the dead and with me"* (Ru 1:8).

It was the right fit. *Ruth clung to her* (Ru 1:14).
They complemented each other and set good ground
rules. Without men to protect them and where women
were considered chattel, they all knew the road ahead
was rough. *Go, return each of you to her mother's house
. . . The Lord grant that you may find a home and rest,
each in the house of her husband! Then she kissed them
and they wept aloud. And they said to her, No, we will
return with you to your people. But Naomi said, Turn
back, my daughters* (Ru 1:8-11). As if they were her
own, she called them both her daughters. As widows,

Naomi had nothing left to offer but the chance for a new life by letting go and encouraging them to re-marry and start over again with a new life. Orpah fi-nally chose to return, but Ruth stayed with Naomi un-derstanding Naomi had nothing to offer for provision other than a deeply held faith in God. *When Naomi saw that Ruth was determined to go with her, she said no more. So they both went on until they came to Beth-lehem* (Ru 1:18-19).

They spoke the truth in love and filled the need in each other to help each other enter the land God was providing for them. It was live or starve. Stripped of all comfort and family, Naomi displayed her raw honesty with heart-breaking emotion, *Call me not Naomi [pleasant]; call me Mara [bitter], for the Almighty has dealt very bitterly with me. I went out full, but the Lord has brought me home again empty. Why call me Naomi, since the Lord has testified against me, and the Almighty has afflicted me?* (Ru 1:20-21).

Naomi showed her unconditional love by calling Ruth her own daughter and holding on to their rela-tionship. *They both went on until they came to Bethle-hem. And they came to Bethlehem at the beginning of barley harvest.* (Ru 1:19,22). *Go, my daughter* (Ru 2:2). And Ruth listened. *And Ruth said to her, All that you say to me I will do* (Ru 3:5). They both held on by let-ting go of their own ways, choosing God's will instead.

Naomi knew she could not provide a family for Ruth, but God could and did. *Have I yet sons in my womb that may become your husband? . . . Would you therefore wait till they were grown?* (Ru 1:11,13). So Naomi and Ruth let God do what they could not. They came to Bethlehem at the beginning of harvest. *And [Ruth] went and gleaned in a field after the reapers; and she happened to stop at the part of the field be-*

longing to Boaz (Ru 2:3). God's coincidence was *meant to be* for Ruth! The same passage in the Tanakh reads, *... she came and gleaned in a field, behind the reapers; and,* **as luck would have it,** *it was the piece of land belonging to Boaz....* (JPS-HET).

So the big picture in the intimate and beautifully portrayed mentored relationship between Naomi and Ruth was God establishing the lineage of Jesus through Ruth and Boaz (see Ru 4:22). Ruth really loved God and wanted to follow Him. She saw the faith Naomi had and wanted it. The strongest tie between Naomi and Ruth was a spiritual one; there their relationship was about a calling of God on their lives that they instinctively knew and were responding to. These timeless tips of mentoring will work for you, too, to paint a picture bigger than you ever dreamed.

Mentoring gave me a pattern of living to follow which held me together so that I could have what I wanted. God let me have what I wanted when He wanted me to have it. He gave me Joy, and He'll take care of the rest. I have to trust Him for the results and be at peace. We wanted our relationship but let God cause the growth. It's all up to Him! He will bring it to pass.

Personal Process Assessment

You have to want it. A point of importunity is the place where you desire something so much, it's like you're drowning in the ocean and you will do anything to get a gulp of air that will save your life. What is your point of importunity? What do you really want?

You need to know what the desire of your heart really is. Don't misplace or misspend your heart's desire, either. So often we are working for something that we think will fill us, but we're just filling the room with more junk. What means more to you than anything else? What is the real desire of your heart? What makes you truly happy?

Sometimes we need to let go of relationships that pull us down by bringing out the worst in us or our situation. Letting go doesn't mean being mean or unforgiving, but rather placing the person and relationship in God's hands and trusting Him for the results. Sometimes we need to detach with love. How important is it? Who makes you happy so you mutually bring out the best in each other?

Tips to Mentoring: How to Find
or Become a Trusted Friend and Advisor

1. Discover Your Heart's Desire
2. Cultivate a Good Friendship
3. Find the Right Fit
4. Complement—Don't Compete With—Each Other
5. Set Good Ground Rules
6. Speak the Truth in Love
7. Find a Need and Fill It
8. Experience Mutual and Unconditional Love
9. Hold on by Letting Go
10. Let Him Do What You Can't

Quality relationships that fit us take time to grow and need good nourishment. Who are those people in your life whom you love and can be real with? What are you doing to nurture the relationship, to complement each other, love, respect, and enjoy each other?

The one thought we want you to hold on to is that mentoring helps you find what you want and encourages you to hold on to your desire until you get it.

If any man desires to do His will (God's pleasure), he will know (have the needed illumination to recognize, and can tell for himself) whether the teaching is from God or whether I am speaking from Myself and of My own accord and on My own authority.

John 7:17

Behold, You desire truth in the inner being; make me therefore to know wisdom in my inmost heart.

Psalm 51:6

Whoever observes the [king's] command will experience no harm, and a wise man's mind will know both when and what to do. For every purpose and matter has its [right] time and judgment, although the misery and wickedness of man lies heavily upon him [who rebels against the king].

Ecclesiastes 8:5-6

He will fulfill the desires of those who reverently and worshipfully fear Him; He also will hear their cry and will save them.

Psalm 145:19

CHAPTER FIVE
Make a Path; Leave a Trail

Hear, O Israel: the Lord our God is one Lord [the only Lord].

Deuteronomy 6:4

In this matter, then, of eating food offered to idols, we know that an idol is nothing (has no real existence) and that there is no God but one.

1 Corinthians 8:4

So God created man in His own image.

Genesis 1:27

That is why I would remind you to stir up (rekindle the embers of, fan the flame of, and keep burning) the [gracious] gift of God, [the inner fire] that is in you by means of the laying on of my hands [with those of the elders at your ordination]. [For it is He] Who delivered and saved us and called us with a calling in itself holy and leading to holiness [to a life of consecration, a vocation of holiness]; [He did it] not because of anything of merit that we have done, but because of and to further His own purpose and grace (unmerited favor) which was given us in Christ Jesus before the world began [eternal ages ago]. [It is that purpose and grace] which He now has made known and has fully disclosed and made real [to us] through the appearing of our Savior Christ Jesus, Who annulled death and made it of no effect and brought life and immortality (immunity from eternal death) to light through the Gospel. Hold fast . . .

2 Timothy 1:6,9,10,13

Do not go where the path may lead,
go instead where there is no path and leave a trail.

Ralph Waldo Emerson

He reached from on high, He took me; He drew me out of many
waters.

Psalm 18:16

You are unique. God made you an individual unlike any other, born with the natural propensity and potential to make your own path. *You sift and search out my path . . . Even the darkness hides nothing from You . . . My frame was not hidden from You when I was being formed in secret [and] intricately and curiously wrought [as if embroidered with various colors] in the depths of the earth [a region of darkness and mystery]. In Your book all the days [of my life] were written before ever they took shape, when as yet there was none of them* (Ps 139:3,12,15,16).

Jesus loves you with an inimitable, authentic love. It is a love second to none. His love for you cannot be imitated or matched by anyone or anything else in the entire universe. His love for you is too good to be copied or equaled.

Authority is a cognate of authentic, and it means the power to influence or command thought. Isn't it amazing to get a little glimpse of the awesomeness of who God is!

God calls you through His love. The more you open your heart and mind to a microscopic semblance of understanding and receiving this love, the more unique you will see that you are. God is love; God is unique. We were made in His likeness, so we are loved and we are unique!

The more you internalize this thought and God's love, the safer you feel and the more you will be drawn to His calling on your life. God's calling card is His love. God calls us into a relationship with Him before He calls us into doing anything for Him.

We have to be drawn by God's love before we can be driven with purpose. I don't have to love Jesus. I want to! When you understand who you are and how loved you are, you will live out a satisfying life by fulfilling your calling. You will find yourself in a class by yourself. This is not about rebellion, as is prevalent in today's culture. It is about being who you are, unlike anyone else. You have your own identity given to you by God Himself.

You shall be called by a new name, which the mouth of the Lord will name (Is 62:2). *I will give him a white stone with a new name engraved on the stone, which no one knows or understands except he who receives it* (Re 2:17). Unique is part of your nature. Through God's love in and through Joy, she loved me and let me be me. In my recovery program, I learn that it's a program of attraction and not promotion. Drawn by the calling literally means to attract by a strong, inner impulse toward a particular course of action, especially when accompanied by conviction of divine influence. I'm more comfortable around authentic people who aren't trying to be something they're not.

Joy mentored me in being unique. It was definitely by divine appointment that we met. God knew I needed her in my life, and I wanted it. I really do believe we were meant to meet, and because of that, her mentoring is divine mentoring, something that was meant to be. Who are the people in your life whom you know are meant to be there?

Being unique is a feeling of greatness. This is not to be confused with a psychological need to be important. Being unique, or having this feeling of greatness, is the foundation upon which your dream is built.

This feeling is a spiritual sixth sense, born in your spirit and not in your emotional realm, although emotions can give strength to this sense. Our uniqueness needs to be called out in each one of us. Joy calls this feeling of greatness the "spark of divinity" (see diagram, page 31).

The spark of divinity is that place in our spirit where God meets man and man meets his dream. Some people see their dreams but never see God. Some see God, but never see their dreams. Some see both. Rachel finds she sees God but not her dream. She holds on to His promises, and this gives her comfort. I believe she is not alone. She is also drawn by God's call on her life.

The feeling of greatness in our spirit is where our destiny lies. It is the spark that ignites the fire. There would be no life without it. It would be like the hull without the seed. None of us really believes we're great in ourselves.

God births in each human being this feeling of greatness which becomes the foundation upon which dreams are built. It is not of us, and that is why it stays in our hearts.

Start with your epitaph. Start with the end in mind. How do you want to be remembered? I want my epitaph to read, "She was lovingkind and wise." This thought subconsciously precludes everything I think and do.

There is only one of you. None of us are alike. Mother Theresa is one of Joy's heroes. Joy could not be like her—nor should she be. However, she can have that same spirit of love. It takes on the form of its possessor and will flow through a willing vessel like water in a pitcher. She needs to be who she is, unique in how she has been shaped by the things in her life that have built into her compassion, concern, and caring for others.

She often wonders what prompted the Good Samaritan who stopped and ministered to the man robbed and beaten. Could it have been the rejection from Israel he had felt as a Samaritan? What about the disciples when through their needs they rose to follow Jesus? They could never be Jesus, but they could have His Spirit.

I can never be Joy, but I can have a spirit like hers. Going from imitation to unique meant learning not to be and do what I perceived others expected of me, but to follow my heart and God's will for me. God's authentic love, working through her, filled my spirit so I might truly love and be whom God made me to be. Her life was an example for me to follow.

Learning has more to do with what is caught than taught. Just as I try to teach my children and pass my life on, so my mentor teaches me and passes her life on. "I can teach my children what I believe, but I reproduce who I am." Joy can teach me all day, but she is passing on to me who she is in Jesus. *He must increase, but I must decrease. [He must grow more prominent; I must grow less so.]* (Jo 3:30). This by no means implies we become the same person. The same spirit of love or character manifests itself according to the personality carrying it. This is what mentoring is all about.

We are each unique. This is part of God's great plan. History repeatedly proves that every great person or leader has been unique. Even the seemingly smaller actions are unique. For example, the woman who poured an alabaster box of precious ointment on Jesus' head as He ate impressed Him. He then declared her action was great: *what this woman has done will be told also, in memory of her* (Ma 26:13).

When God made you, He threw the mold away. DNA says the same thing. The circumstances and events that take place in our lives help make us who we are and bring out the unique qualities in each of us. God reveals His love for us through these experiences. They define us and impel us to do certain things or to take a particular path.

Moses was a unique man who took a unique path and was a unique mentor. Moses' name means "one who draws out." *Pharaoh's daughter . . . called him Moses, for she said, Because I drew him out of the water* (Ex 2:10). While all the Hebrew male infants were thrown into the Nile, *by faith Moses, after his birth, was kept concealed for three months by his parents, because they saw how comely the child was; and they were not overawed and terrified by the king's decree* (He 11:23).

Moses' life is an extraordinary example of health and well-being into old age, and yet he lived one of the most stressful lives in history. He was responsible for the downfall of Pharaoh. Single-handedly but supernaturally, Moses helped his own nation out of bondage to Egypt and took them into uncharted territory and freedom with outstanding opposition from only his own people and his own family.

Hebrews 11:25-27 makes it abundantly clear how important his path was to him. *Because he preferred to share the oppression [suffer the hardships] and bear the shame of the people of God rather than to have the fleeting enjoyment of a sinful life. He considered the contempt and abuse and shame [borne for] the Christ (the Messiah Who was to come) to be greater wealth than all the treasures of Egypt, for he looked forward and away to the reward (recompense). [Motivated] by faith he left Egypt behind him, being unawed and undismayed by the wrath of the king; for he never flinched but held staunchly to his purpose and endured steadfastly as one who gazed on Him Who is invisible.*

He left everything he held dear for a relationship with God. He knew God loved him. He was drawn by God's call. After leading his people out of unimaginable oppression, he watched them revolt against their own freedom, against God, and die in the desert. In spite of such overwhelming odds, constant life-and-death conflict, he survived being in the presence of God; he saw God's commands crumble and rebuild.

Moses was one of the greatest leaders the world has ever seen, yet he was a very humble man. He went from riches to rags for the sake of God's destiny and purpose in his life, which was rooted in God's calling. He woke up each day with purpose, finding meaning in all the circumstances God had for him. God showed His way to Moses. *He made known His ways [of righteousness and justice] to Moses* (Ps 103:7).

Moses blazed a unique path but left a trail for Joshua to follow. They were both following God's call on their lives. *Moses was 120 years old when he died; his eye was not dim nor his natural force abated* (De 34:7). *Joshua son of Nun was full of the spirit of wisdom, for Moses had laid his hands upon him* (De 34:9). Joshua was Moses' personal attendant throughout the 40 years in the wilderness. He was with Moses on the mount and was one of the 12 spies sent out by Moses to scout out the land of Canaan. Like Moses, Joshua trusted and prayed to God. What an incomparable example of divine mentoring!

Love precludes unique. Understanding how much Jesus loves you gives you the courage to be yourself. Moses and Joshua knew how much God loved them. Joy and I love God immensely. Our love and enjoyment of Him is probably our greatest common bond. We had this in common before we met, and God knew this, of course.

What is your God concept? Our God concept is

rooted in our internalized thoughts and feelings about our earthly father. If we have a good and healthy relationship with our earthly father, we likely will have good feelings about our heavenly Father. If we experienced an unhealthy, negative or nonexistent relationship with our earthly father, we probably will have a hard time trusting our heavenly Father. The good news is that as we allow the process of trust to develop, God will re-create through our experiences with Him a positive God concept.

When his heart disease almost took his life, Zach encountered a metamorphosis in his God concept. The rigid, legalistic God in his mind transformed into a living, loving God through His Word, in prayer, and in the events that transformed his life. He saw how much God loved him in every detail that occurred.

Zach was humbled by what he went through and grateful for what took the place of his former life. Humility was one of his greatest lessons learned. "When I think of humility, I think of it as the 'Eleventh Commandment,' in respect to God's omnipotence and omnipresence. Being humbled brought forth in me a passionate love. I know it sounds funny, but I passionately love God.

"When we had this baby, I never thought I could love her the way I do. When I mentioned that to my beloved and beautiful wife, she made a very profound statement: 'God loves that baby more than you do.' I thought about that for a minute, and I thought about the expansiveness and intensity of God's love, the love that was demonstrated when His Son was butchered on the cross. As a mere mortal thinking about how much I love this baby, to think that He has the capacity to love that baby more than I do, it humbles me.

"And to know that He personally loves me that much intensifies and edifies my focus on the Holy

Trinity and what I'm doing. It motivates me to give back and to love Him. The two commandments that Christ said were the most important are to love Him and love others. I am not a social person. I often feel uncomfortable around other people, but I love and give back because I passionately love God."

Jesus loves you so very much. There simply aren't enough words to describe how much He cares, how far He will go, or how much He will do for you. You have to let Him. You have to experience this for yourself. Jesus' love for you is second to none.

Defining moments show your uniqueness. A defining moment births in you a desire that determines or directs your destiny. It may be a recurring event or a one-time experience. It may be positive, but it is often negative. The decisions you make as a result may be conscious or unconscious. Regardless of what happened or whether you are aware of the decisions you've made as a result, a defining moment has made its indelible imprint on you.

A defining moment is like a load-bearing wall in the house. There may be more than one, but a load-bearing wall in a house is always part of the foundation and supports the structure. Just as these walls that sustain the construction of a house, there are defining moments that support the structure of our lives.

Sometimes forgotten or not realized, we eventually recall them. However, what is of paramount importance is not the event itself but how we choose to respond to it. Choice is God's gift to you.

Our helplessness doesn't disconnect us from the power these events have had over our lives. In my 12-step program, I have learned my helplessness is the very thing that brings me life. *Have mercy on me and be gracious to me, O Lord, for I am weak (faint and withered away); O Lord, heal me, for my bones are troubled. My [inner] self [as well as my body] is also exceedingly disturbed and troubled. But You, O Lord, how long [until You return and speak peace to me]? Return [to my relief], O Lord, deliver my life; save me for the sake of Your steadfast love and mercy* (Ps 6:2-4).

Step One: acknowledging my powerlessness over whatever rules me, that only God can restore me to sanity. *When He saw the throngs, He was moved with pity and sympathy for them, because they were bewildered (harassed and distressed and dejected and helpless), like sheep without a shepherd* (Ma 9:36). Jesus understands and knows how I feel.

Step One is the only step I can actually take. Steps two through twelve, God has to do through me. In the rooms of recovery, I have learned this and incorporated new habits through working my program and sponsorship.

Recovery is such an important part of being unique because it gives us permission to individuate and be all who God meant us to be. *I will not leave you as orphans [comfortless, desolate, bereaved, forlorn, helpless]; I will come [back] to you* (Jo 14:18). Jesus meets us in recovery. Recovery teaches us boundaries: where I end and another person begins. Defining moments help us draw boundaries around who we are.

Sponsorship is mentoring in recovery. As a vital part of the 12-step program, we are encouraged to find someone who has been successfully working the program, and with whom we can identify and confide. This enables us to be accountable in a way that encourages our growth through this mentoring relationship. We are only as sick as our secrets, and unloading our secrets and our shame in a safe way is one of the greatest gifts in sponsorship. It is also one of the key reasons sponsorship works so well. It is a win-win relationship in a class by itself.

I improve faster with a sponsor. I grow stronger spiritually as a sponsor. Often my sponsor would see a unique gift in me that I was unable to see in myself. My friend, whom I sponsored, saw herself through completely different eyes than I did until she started accepting her good traits as well as her character defects. I saw her gifts, the unique strengths she was oblivious to. What we feed grows, and in either capacity we are strengthening those principles that prevent us from sabotaging our own success.

What impels you? Defining moments determine our destiny by bringing to light and life those predestined gifts God gave you. They come to fruition through the experiences of life.

Joy's moment of impact was when she went into her bedroom and prayed for an understanding heart to help people who are hurting. She wanted to go to the medicine cabinet and poison her stepfather but instead made a different choice.

She knew Jesus loved her. She knew He loved her like none other. Her emotions added strength to her decision. Joy was and still is impelled to help hurting people until it is time for her to leave this earth.

In his landmark *Man's Search for Meaning,* Viktor E. Frankl said, ". . . Everything can be taken from a man but one thing—the last of the human freedoms—to choose one's attitude in any given set of circumstances, to choose one's own way." This incredible and unusual Jewish psychiatrist survived Auschwitz and saw horrific human misery. He found that what kept people alive in the prison camps had nothing to do with status, wealth, or even health. What kept them going were relationships. If a husband was living for his wife and she died, he would die soon after.

The Holocaust was his defining moment that revealed his purpose. While in the death camp, he envisioned himself speaking to huge conferences on what he experienced and endured. He is the founder of "logo therapy" or "the will to meaning," one of the world's most effective treatments for mental illness. It helps the patient find the will to live one's life. Just as emotions add strength to decisions, so purpose fuels goals. The more meaningful the purpose, the more motivated you are to reach your goals.

Our brain is like a computer, constantly processing information, placing it and categorizing it. This is why it is so important to understand the brain's process. Understanding paves the way to living the most meaningful life possible. *But when He, the Spirit of Truth (the Truth-giving Spirit) comes, He will guide you into all the Truth (the whole, full Truth)* (Jo 16:13).

Joy's defining moment with her stepfather inspired her to help people. This moment also incited her to hate him. Appendicitis was a defining moment that validated both positive and negative decisions Joy made—her desire to comfort others and her judgment regarding her stepfather.

Once the forgiveness process was put in place, her defining moments were used to fuel the purpose in her life instead of the hatred in her heart. Joy's heart realized, "There but for the grace of God, go I."

God uses these defining moments to bring forth gifts He has already given you. They come to fruition through the experiences of life. Are you being inspired or incited by these pivotal points in time?

Joy was on the right track defining her destiny but still had to remove some obstacles in the road ahead. God in His grace was directing Joy's destiny in spite of her attitude toward her stepfather.

So often we are acutely aware of an area that needs

to be addressed but feel that thing is preventing us from being, having, or doing what we were meant to. Understanding the significance of your defining moments will help you clarify your life's meaning. What meaningful friendships in your life seem set apart? Why are they distinctive? Do you see God's love in them? How have you been enriched with their wisdom and insight—or how have you shared your wisdom and counsel?

The gifts and callings of God are irrevocable. They are already there waiting to be worked out. Drugs and alcohol may mask a personality with a costume of deceit, but recovery calls forth the real person as the fading effects of chemicals lose their hold. You are unique. You were born a certain way, and the circumstances of your life will bring it out.

Jake knew Jesus as his Savior but didn't make Jesus his Lord until he got into recovery for the alcoholism that was gripping his life. Drawn by a calling from God to help the utterly helpless, Jake literally saves the lives of men who are dying in the streets from chemical abuse.

As a sponsor for other recovering alcoholics, Jake daily sees the fruit of sponsorship in the men he mentors. Sponsorship is mentoring in recovery. In certain recovery meetings, there are monthly workshops designed to help people just coming off the street. They've stopped drugging and drinking, but their chemical equilibrium is still off balance. They're looking for something to replace the drugs and alcohol.

In the first week of the workshop, one half of the room is people who are "clean" and in recovery. The other half is people just off the streets. Jake and the other leaders ask, "If you are here to do the 12 steps of recovery, to be taken through the steps, please stand up." The street people stand and one by one, each one will be paired with a sober, recovered person. The leaders will look at the group and say, "We need a man." And then a man who has experience and who has been through the workshop will say, "I'll take him." They make eye contact, pair up, and after the session they exchange phone numbers and go through the monthly workshop together.

Jake explained, "Sponsorship in this setting is mentoring with a conscious commitment. You know who the mentor is, and the mentored is someone who recognizes their need and is willing to walk through whatever they need to with another person who shares the life inside of them. The sponsors pass their lives on to the person in need. Typically people who are coming to the workshop are struggling. They're hurting. They're cognizant that alcoholism is causing problems in their lives, so they're more open-minded and willing to listen and learn at that point. Because the narcissistic subconscious ego is now at the point of deflation, whether it's just in a state of compliance or a state of surrender remains to be seen.

"So when we're in that state of surrender, that's the hope. That's the gift because it is a gift. Through our surrender we experience the presence of God, and now that we are clean, God can flow through us." Jake understands that sponsorship in the recovery program is vital because it keeps both the sponsor and the newcomer sober by living out a surrendered life.

Through sponsorship, people get to know each other at a deeper level; they find a safe haven in which to vent their feelings and experiences, and as a result, the real person comes forth. People learn to love each other. Becoming who God meant you to be is a natural consequence of this process. Feeling safe enough to be yourself gives you the confidence to express what is in you. You just need to be willing.

Another defining moment for Joy was her heart being healed when she was 34 years old. She had to recognize her own willingness to do whatever it took to be part of God's plan—to live or die. She felt how much Jesus loves her.

This significant event developed in her a strength that still supports her today. She learned to keep her priorities in balance. She didn't sacrifice her children for the sake of ministry. Her experiences taught her how to be secure in God's love for her; she didn't let people dictate her attitude or actions.

When her son Tommy was not even six years old, Joy recalls an incident that challenged her church commitment. It was a defining moment for them both. Tommy came into the house carrying a boat that was a recent gift from a friend.

"Oh, mother," he exclaimed. "I just love this little ship, but I don't have any place to sail it." He had his mother's tenacity. "Mother, can we go to Slope Park and sail it?"

"But, honey, we have church tonight," Joy hesitated. "And it's already afternoon." She thought about it. "We would have to go by street car or trolley. I just don't know if we have the time."

"Mother, I really need to do this." Joy looked at her little son telling her it was so important to him.

She went for it. They got to Slope Park, Tommy sailed his little ship on that beautiful afternoon, and they returned just in time for church that evening.

It's the little things in life that count, and Tommy never forgot that moment. One of the greatest leaders in ministry today learned that he was more important to his mother than church was. He understood in his mother's eyes, and in God's, he was second to none.

"Uniqueness is a quality that draws out the real person. When you see a person who is unique, you know that is a sign that God is there," states Joy. Unique is about being authentic.

Authenticity is the reflection of the feeling of greatness. The feeling of greatness is a portion of God's spirit implanted in every human being. *The spirit of man [that factor in human personality which proceeds immediately from God] is the lamp of the Lord, searching all his innermost parts* (Pr 20:27). It is a little spark of divinity given by God. *For what person perceives (knows and understands) what passes through a man's thoughts except the man's own spirit within him? Just so no one discerns (comes to know and comprehend) the thoughts of God except the Spirit of God* (1 Co 2:11). This sense or feeling of greatness is something that cannot be stolen or duplicated by anybody.

Instead of being like everyone else, the spark of divinity calls you to be unique, unlike anyone else. *He Who began a good work in you will continue until the day of Jesus Christ [right up to the time of His return], developing [that good work] and perfecting and bringing it to full completion in you* (Ph 1:6). We are each born with certain tendencies or qualities, and God enhances those by sending experiences into life to help accentuate that uniqueness, to point it out and show the way. *The Lord will perfect that which concerns me; Your mercy and loving-kindness, O Lord, endure forever—forsake not the works of Your own hands* (Ps 138:8).

In her counseling, Joy found that inside each person, there is a feeling of greatness. She used to think this was just in certain people, but she learned that each person has this. Sometimes you have to dig deep to find it, no matter what seems to be covering it. It only needs to be uncovered, awakened.

While living in Florida, I bought two bougainvilleas and potted them in white planters on either side of my front door, facing east. I was tired of replacing the flowers in the pots every four months, so I tried something a little more permanent, especially since my thumb isn't particularly green. The bougainvillea blooms a beautiful fuchsia pink flower. But the only fuchsia blooms I saw on those bougainvilleas for three years were the ones that were there when I first bought the plants. And they certainly weren't permanent.

After the third spring, I finally gave up on those bougainvilleas at the front door, but I didn't discard them because they weren't dead. The landscaper said they needed to be in a sunnier spot. So I moved them to the end of the pool facing west. And sure enough, within two months, one of them started to bloom, then the other!

Hurricane Irene howled through the following October with gale force winds ravaging our property, including those two bougainvilleas and a 12-foot tall, 15-year-old bougainvillea in the back yard. In spite of the advice given by a nursery owner to "get rid of them all" and start over, I once again chose to keep them and give them another chance. I left alone the two near the pool and had huge supports put around the old bougainvillea, which must have lost thousands of flowers.

Within the year, all three bougainvilleas had more gorgeous fuchsia pink flowers than anyone would ever be able to count. When I mentioned this to the landscaper one afternoon, he remarked offhandedly that he had seen a lot of plants struggle to "make it." And in all his years of working with plants, the plants that were damaged the most and really struggled and had to fight to survive ended up blooming better and became the prettiest, strongest, and hardiest plants. *I planted, Apollos watered, but God [all the while] was making it grow and [He] gave the increase. So neither he who plants is anything nor he who waters, but [only] God Who makes it grow and become greater* (1 Co 3:6-7).

As you walk and work through your own personal process, you will find the consummation of your own uniqueness coming forth, unlike any other. There is greatness inside of you. It is God's little spark of divinity that ignites the fire in you.

Personal Process Assessment

You are second to none. You are unique, and you were born with the propensity to make your own path. What makes you different than anybody else? How are you unique? How are you free to express yourself?

God calls you through His love. The more you internalize this thought and let it seep into your spirit, the more you will be drawn to God. When we feel loved, we feel safe enough to be who God meant us to be. How do you make others feel safe? Who makes you feel safe? Do you feel drawn to God calling you?

Mentoring ignites the spark and fuels the fire. It is most effective when rooted in God's love. Love does not demand its own way. Which friendships in your life are second to none? What makes them unique?

Jesus loves you with a love second to none. Jesus loves you with a love that cannot be matched or imitated in all life. Close your eyes for a moment and reflect on this. Think of how much He loves only you. How have you experientially felt, seen, or understood Jesus' love for you?

I felt His unconditional love when Joy told me she'd love me even if I was in prison for murder. The best way she could describe how much she cared was to think of me in the worst way possible. Which friendships in your life demonstrate this depth of love?

The spark of divinity is that place in our spirit where God meets you and you meet your dream, calling, or purpose. The gifts and calling of God are irrevocable. They are already there waiting to be worked out. *For God's gifts and His call are irrevocable. [He never withdraws them when once they are given, and He does not change His mind about those to whom He gives His grace or to whom He sends His call]* (Ro 11:29). Some people see their dreams and callings but never see God. Some see God but never see their dreams. Some see both. Have you seen your spark of divinity?

You are unique, your calling is unique, and mentoring brings it out. In which friendships do you feel safe enough to be yourself? Who brings out the best in you? Do you bring out the best in your friends?

God is love; God is unique; you were made in His likeness. God loves you with an authentic love, and He made you unique! God, His love, and you are second to none!

Now about food offered to idols: of course we know that all of us possess knowledge [concerning these matters. Yet mere] knowledge causes people to be puffed up (to bear themselves loftily and be proud), but love (affection and goodwill and benevolence) edifies and builds up and encourages one to grow [to his full stature].

1 Corinthians 8:1

Go confidently in the direction of your dream.
Live the life you have imagined.

Henry David Thoreau

And your ears will hear a word behind you, saying,
This is the way; walk in it,
when you turn to the right hand
and when you turn to the left.

Isaiah 30:21

But if one loves God truly [with affectionate reverence, prompt
obedience, and grateful recognition of His blessing], he is known
by God [recognized as worthy of His intimacy and love, and he is
owned by Him].

1 Corinthians 8:3

Worthy are You, our Lord and God, to receive the glory and the
honor and dominion, for You created all things; by Your will they
were [brought into being] and were created.

Revelation 4:11

Deserving is the Lamb, Who was sacrificed, to receive all the
power and riches and wisdom and might and honor and majesty
(glory, splendor) and blessing!
And I heard every created thing in heaven and on earth and
under the earth [in Hades, the place of departed spirits] and
on the sea and all that is in it, crying out together, To Him Who
is seated on the throne and to the Lamb be ascribed the
blessing and the honor and the majesty (glory, splendor) and
the power (might and dominion) forever and ever (through
the eternities of the eternities)!

Revelation 5:12-13

CHAPTER SIX
Lessons Learned

I [the Lord] will instruct you and teach you in the way you should go; I will counsel you with My eye upon you. Be not like the horse or the mule, which lack understanding, which must have their mouths held firm with bit and bridle, or else they will not come with you.

Psalm 32:8-9

*Oil and perfume rejoice the heart;
so does the sweetness of a friend's counsel
that comes from the heart.*

Proverbs 27:9

*I hear and I forget.
I see and I remember.
I do and I know how.*

Anonymous

More is caught than taught. In every lesson I learned from Joy, she never spoke it. She lived it. And if repetition is the mother of learning, then mentoring is the most conducive conduit of learning.

Joy consistently used fundamental principles of living that I'd catch and put into practice in my own life. These were lessons that I needed to learn.

Although each person's journey is different, the basic fundamental needs of all of us remain constant. So many mentoring moments made engrafting life principles into my soul so simple because Joy and I enjoyed each other so much.

We continue to be the best of friends, and I listen to her with both ears open and ready. Joy and I don't just talk. We communicate. We listen and we understand each other. Always, what amazes me the most is her humble spirit that says she still has so far to go, that she hasn't "made it."

Joy has fueled the fire in my soul and passed the torch of her life on to me in so many ways. I did have to be built up and mature enough to carry the torch. Jesus said, *I have still many things to say to you, but you are not able to bear them or to take them upon you or to grasp them now* (Jo 16:12).

Mentoring and sponsoring share the dynamics of life flowing through relationships like an electrical current that brings light. Joy's life manifests through me by His peace reflecting in my countenance. Last Christmas it took three extension cords to reach a tree at the end of the driveway that I wanted lit for the holidays. Jesus is the Life, and Joy and I are the extension cords that reach out to Rachel. What means the most to Rachel is lending a listening ear without any imposed judgment. Sponsorship is the same principle as mentoring and is so effective in recovery because it operates in an accountable setting. It is wise to have a sponsor who has a sponsor because then they are dealing with their issues and not keeping it in the dark. We are only as sick as our secrets, so keeping our behavior accountable, especially where it has been dysfunctional, keeps us healthy mentally and spiritually. Sponsorship is such a prime example of spiritual growth and fruit bearing because it operates in a secure setting and you have to make a conscious commitment. Often Christian discipleship fails when there is the start of a good friendship but no follow-through.

With two very dear Christian friends, we covenanted our relationship. We made a conscious commitment to each other, discussed the consequences, and agreed years ago to be there for each other. From the beginning, it was the right fit for the three of us. We have a lot in common: a deep and lasting love for Jesus, similar value systems, children, kids' activities, working husbands while we're stay-at-home moms, Bible studies, shopping, lunches, volunteers at school, church and wherever else God wants us.

We go to different churches and live in different places but are close and loyal to each other without control, gossip or condemnation. We listen with a lot of love and understanding and without judgment, give each other permission to fail, encourage each other, experience the good and bad consequences of our decisions, and help pick each other up. We don't talk about each other behind each other's back; we go straight to each other when we feel the need, work through any issues without letting them fester.

We've mentored each other in those areas wherever whoever has experience, maturity, strength and hope. These deep, fulfilling relationships have made life much more meaningful for us together and individually, keeping us close to each other and closer to Jesus.

My 12-step program taught me that alcoholism's influence is contagious. So is recovery. Joy's wisdom and love was and continues to be contagious. I have caught so much love and wisdom from her in our friendship over the years and have passed it on to my loved ones and friends.

We remember what we see longer than what we hear. Michael Deaver, one of the most successful public relations mavericks, was paid well to make President Ronald Reagan look good. He knew people would remember what they saw far longer than what they heard. He didn't care what the media said about the president as long as Reagan was pictured in upbeat patriotic settings, preferably with American flags around him. Deaver wanted to make sure Ronald Reagan's spirit was portrayed for what it was. All those around the president caught his contagious, benevolent spirit. He lived it and passed it on.

The following principles are the top ten things I "caught" from Joy.

1. Be Myself

A truthful witness saves lives, but a deceitful witness speaks lies [and endangers lives]. (Pr 14:25).

Joy is and always has been . . . herself. She is authentic. She's never spoken a "churchy" language, nor has she ever strived to be anyone other than who she is. Even being a pastor's wife for 44 years, she did not fall into the trap or temptation to be or act like someone she wasn't.

She didn't live out the role of someone she thought she ought to be. She was definitely the real diamond and not a cubic zirconium.

Even though I always appreciated and wanted "real," a leadership role offered many alternatives to authentic that looked good but were not necessarily good to the core. We connected in the real zone, and she unconsciously gave me permission to be authentic.

Joy reminded me, "You know any time that we want to be or think we want to be just like somebody else, we're setting ourselves up to be an imitation. I refuse to be that. And I've learned to look past the flaws in leadership—people with great callings but personal weaknesses.

"It used to be so confusing to believe one thing, yet see something else. I really struggled with this issue in prayer, and finally God told me if He doesn't use imperfect people, He won't have anyone. The imperfections in someone else's life are God's business and not mine. He will take care of that. God does not have an inferiority complex."

2. Live an Attitude of Forgiveness

Then Peter came up to Him and said, Lord, how many times may my brother sin against me and I forgive him and let it go? [As many as] up to seven times? Jesus answered him, I tell you, not up to seven times, but seventy times seven! (Ma 18:21-22).

Joy taught me that forgiveness is not just an act; it is an attitude that precedes the act. I learned that nothing has happened to me that is so horrific that I cannot work through the process of forgiveness.

Because I understand the process of forgiveness, I know that part of the process is feeling the hurt of the offense. This is so important because it gives me permission to be real about whatever went on between me and others.

I need to pardon the person, but not the evil. When I keep those boundaries clear, I am also preventing myself from becoming a victim since I see the difference between hating the sin and loving the sinner. What I like best about living an attitude of forgiveness is that it prevents the tough knocks of life from controlling me. Forgiveness keeps hurt from becoming a sin in my own life.

Joy remembers, "My daughter Vicki and I were at a funeral home for somebody at the church, so of course I knew all the people. I'd been the pastor's wife for 44 years. I was standing in front talking to some of the family when I looked at the door and this woman, this mean woman with the most caustic tongue, came walking down to view the body . . . down where I was.

"I panicked, 'What am I going to do?' She got closer and closer, and then she was there. I know the Holy Spirit prompted me to do what happened next.

"She shook my hand, and I said, 'Oh, no. I want a hug.'

"I hugged her, and she said, 'Oh, Sister Barnett, I'm so ashamed at the way I have acted, please forgive me.' She tearfully continued, 'I haven't been the right kind of person to you.'

"I just hugged her a little more tenderly and replied, 'Honey, that wasn't the real you, that was just something that happened and it just does things to us sometimes. Don't even think about that.'

"And I don't think it was the real her. I think the devil was using her emotions to say such mean things.

"That woman became my friend, but I didn't want to forgive her. Denying the pain of a wrong done to you won't do any good. You have to feel the hurt and leave it with Jesus. Sometimes the deeper the pain, the more work that needs to be done, especially if it was something that went on for a long time. As soon as an offense comes, I let it go immediately because if you harbor it, then it's twice as hard to let go. I have not been able to do that entirely yet, but I'm working on it, so it will become natural with me."

3. Emotions Strengthen My Decisions

And Jesus prayed, Father, forgive them, for they know not what they do. And they divided His garments and distributed them by casting lots for them (Lk 23:34).

Jesus didn't say much dying on the cross, so these few words must be really important. He understood the importance of using emotions to understand our actions. These words can motivate our behavior unless it comes to light. Sometimes we don't see the consequences of our behavior until we feel its effects. Joy and my recovery program are what finally gave me permission to feel my feelings.

Joy taught me to use my emotions as an indicator of what's really going on inside my heart. Webster's Dictionary defines emotion as "the state or capability of having feelings aroused to the point of awareness." Joy showed me that this is the way God intended emotions in my life to be used. They aren't meant to rule me, nor am I supposed to suppress them; they are a gift from God, letting me know what's going on in my life.

Years ago, a psychiatrist prescribed for me an antidepressant for reactionary depression. I went to fill it at the little pharmacy in The Plains, Virginia, where everyone knows everyone else. As I handed the pharmacist the prescription slip to fill, he quietly proceeded to tell me about all this particular drug's pitfalls and possible kidney problems that could result. I can't remember what the drug's name was, but I do remember being so scared about taking it, I left the pharmacy without the prescription. Instead, I went into three months of intensive therapy and joined a recovery program, which changed my life. I was in a black hole, and I needed something to help me out. I was willing to do whatever it took to get help.

Statistics show these drugs, when coupled with therapy, are often helpful in restoring a lost sense of well being. Behavior impacts chemical equilibrium in your brain. From the day an alcoholic stops drinking, it takes three to five years for the chemical balance to be restored in the brain. This is why the proper drug can be so effective with therapy; you are retraining your brain. For me, three months of intense therapy with a Holy Spirit-filled, recovering alcoholic, Catholic priest brought healing that is lasting a lifetime.

In most states, psychologists cannot prescribe drugs, only psychiatrists or M.D.s. Also, most psychiatrists only prescribe drugs. Antidepressants are often needed. However, for a lasting change, the person taking the medication should also consider therapy from a psychologist, counselor, or trained pastor. God uses medical progresses to enable us to be all He means us to be. Learning to listen and not react to my emotions has been a major part of recovery and is an ongoing process for me.

There are some medical conditions where drugs are absolutely necessary and may be so for a lifetime. Joy has seen magical transformations take place in people who are able to function normally and be rational after use. God uses these drugs and medical technology to help us and enable us to be all He meant us to be.

Joy's stepfather had an emotional problem, not Joy. It became Joy's problem when she reacted. When she learned to listen to her emotions and not let them rule her, they gave her the impetus and strength to acknowledge and accept the pain of the offense, draw boundaries with him, and forgive him. If you don't feel strongly, how will you carry it out?

"I was talking to God and asking Him, 'Isn't there a place for emotions? You gave us emotions for a purpose. Help me to understand why.'

"He taught me that emotions give force to my decisions. You know what you feel when you channel it in the right direction. Those emotions give force or strength to that channeling. We don't just discount emotions. We know that they do have value because God gave them to us, but we have to use them for the right reasons."

4. When I Abide in Christ, He Answers My Prayers

If you live in Me [abide vitally united to Me] and My words remain in you and continue to live in your hearts, ask whatever you will, and it shall be done for you (Jo 15:7).

He will answer my prayers because He said so. But I must be abiding in Him. The result of abiding in Him is that my will is lining up with His will. There is no one who loves my children more than Jesus. He loves them and desires their salvation more than I do. So I pray for them faithfully and with assurance that when I trust God for their souls, they are in the best of care.

I pray the 4 C's: that God will:

1. **Create** a hunger and thirst for righteousness in their souls,
2. **Convict** them of sin,
3. **Convert** them, and finally
4. Jesus brings them to **Commitment**.

This is My commandment: that you love one another [just] as I have loved you. No one has greater love [no one has shown stronger affection] than to lay down (give up) his own life for his friends. You are My friends if you keep on doing the things which I command you to do (Jo 15:12-14). If I want what He wants, I will be praying for what He wants, so of course He will answer my prayers. My answered prayers are simply the consequence of abiding in Jesus.

"I am the branch on the Vine, and Jesus, Himself, is the Vine flowing through me; that makes me a child of God in the sense that when I pray, the Father sees me as Jesus. When He sees me in the righteousness of His own Son, He will not deny me. I know God is wonderful and that He loves me.

"Years ago, at a pivotal moment in time during prayer, I felt the Word become *rhema* in my spirit. *If you live in Me [abide vitally united to Me] and My words remain in you and continue to live in your hearts, ask whatever you will, and it shall be done for you* (Jo 15:7). They were just words before, but I suddenly realized that this really is the truth.

"I abide in Jesus. I'm the branch growing from the Vine, which is Jesus, and He, Himself flows through me. And when I speak to the Father, He sees me as He sees Jesus. That's the way I learned to pray when I understood who I was in His sight, and here I am because of Him. When you are actually awakened to the fact that the Life of the Vine is in you, what happens is that it becomes a healing flow. It's a renewing flow, an understanding flow that keeps me safe. I understand who I am, because I know Who is in me. Anyone can have this; it doesn't matter who your earthly father is."

5. Listen with My Heart

I said in my haste and alarm, I am cut off from before Your eyes. But You heard the voice of my supplications when I cried to You for aid (Ps 31:22).

God heard the cry of David's heart. I had to learn to listen with my heart. As silly as this sounds, trusting God to a greater degree helped me be a better listener. Turning things over to Him emptied me of my own agenda. Trusting Joy took time as our friendship deepened.

The safer I felt with Joy, the more I emptied myself of my own agenda, opened up to her, and let her in. As I let her in, I listened more with my ears and less with my own thoughts and perceptions. As I did this with her, I did this with my own loved ones and friends.

Joy would always say, "Listening felt like love." She

felt validated, and this is what I have learned to do in my own life. Joy was never afraid to hear anything I had to say.

One day I called her, so angry with myself and heartbroken over something I had done. I can't remember what it was, but I remember the result of talking with Joy and emptying my soul to her.

She listened quietly to my every word, and when I was finished, she kindly replied, "Oh, Lindsey! Why honey, if you told me you had killed someone, I would love you no matter what."

Her words made an indelible imprint on my soul forever. Her heart spoke louder than any words. She knew I felt so much hurt and shame in that moment, and that's what I needed to be set free of.

What is more outstanding is that Joy probably doesn't even remember saying this—not because she is 86, but because this is who Joy is and God's love just flows from her. I was being taught and healed at the same time.

"The word 'feeling' is woven into each memory. Children retain more from what they have sensed than from any word they have heard. It has been well said that it is not what actually happens to a child as how the child feels about it. More is caught than taught."

6. Keep a "Yes! Now!" Attitude

For as many as are the promises of God, they all find their Yes [answer] in Him [Christ]. For this reason we also utter the Amen (so be it) to God through Him [in His Person and by His agency] to the glory of God (2 Co 1:20) . . . behold, now is the day of salvation! (2 Co 6:2).

God is a "Yes, Now" God, and Joy is a "Yes, Now"

person. I am learning to be, and I love it! Find the good and build on it *now*! Joy doesn't let much grass grow under her feet. The spirit world is the present world.

So often in my more immature days, when I would start complaining about something small that seemed so big to me, Joy would listen, then as a friend and not a teacher, would reply, "Oh honey, you'll work it out." In other words, "Get over it. You'll be fine." She took the self-pity right out of me!

I am so good at making mountains out of molehills; I was crowding my life with unimportant things and taking the fun and effectiveness out of living for my loved ones and myself.

How important is it? If it isn't, I will let go of it and focus on what counts and is really important. She was always finding the good, building on it, and throwing out the trash. Joy effectively showed me how to do the same.

"Ladies, we are the enhancers. We set the atmosphere in the home. Being a godly mother is not about us. We are in the family to make our husbands great. We are in the family to make our children great. When we do this it influences generation after generation, and our husbands and our children will rise up and call us blessed."

7. God Leads Me Down Unchosen Paths

A man's mind plans his way, but the Lord directs his steps and makes them sure (Pr 16:9).

Sometimes I may want to be or do something because it's the closest thing that will fulfill my dream. Then I end up doing something different, but it's really what I was meant to do. Because when my will lines up with God's will, the dream becomes the calling. God was grooming me all along. Roadblocks are often building blocks for the future.

"If you really dig, and if you really listen to the things that happen to you in life, they are the things that God is using to reveal to you the direction He is taking you. If you understood the directions totally, they wouldn't have value. But God is trying to mold the inner person, the concept, the drive, the force.

"Feeling and experiencing these things fulfills the destiny that God has for you. And as you do this step-by-step, the Holy Spirit is moving you to that defining moment. He helps you make a decision and stick with it. It will not leave you because God birthed it in you from the very beginning. The qualities that you need to fulfill your destiny come to fruition, and God has led you through these steps to try to point it out to you.

"In this final great moment of impact, God has given you understanding. When I am led down this path I did not plan to go, I know it is the Hand of God."

8. Give What I Don't Have

Now the wife of a son of the prophets cried to Elisha, Your servant my husband is dead, and you know that your servant feared the Lord. But the creditor has come to take my two sons to be his slaves.

Elisha said to her, What shall I do for you? Tell me, what have you [of sale value] in the house? She said, Your handmaid has nothing in the house except a jar of oil.

Then he said, Go around and borrow vessels from all your neighbors, empty vessels—and not a few.

And when you come in, shut the door upon you and your sons. Then pour out [the oil you have] into all those vessels, setting aside each one when it is full.

So she went from him and shut the door upon herself and her sons, who brought to her the vessels as she poured the oil.

When the vessels were all full, she said to her son, Bring me another vessel. And he said to her, There is not a one left. Then the oil stopped multiplying.

Then she came and told the man of God. He said, Go, sell the oil and pay your debt, and you and your sons live on the rest.

2 Kings 4:1-7

This story holds relevant and significant symbolism for women today. Any woman who is single, has lost her husband through death or divorce, or has an absent husband due to service, work, or other circumstances, can feel the depth of this woman's vulnerability. Both Joy and I married men whose positions kept them away from home frequently. This gave us profound compassion and understanding for each other.

Joy lived by the principles in this story that kept this woman and her offspring blessed by God. She believed the glass was half full and not half empty. What you feed grows, and she fed thoughts of ample supply and not inadequate lack. She stayed close to God's church, and she was obedient and trusted God in her time of greatest need when things looked the worst. *[Remember] this: he who sows sparingly and grudgingly will also reap sparingly and grudgingly, and he who sows generously [that blessings may come to someone] will also reap generously and with blessings. Let each one [give] as he has made up his own mind and purposed in his heart, not reluctantly or sorrowfully or under compulsion, for God loves (He takes pleasure in, prizes above other things, and is unwilling to abandon or to do without) a cheerful (joy-*

*ous, "prompt to do it") giver [whose heart is in his giv-
ing]* (2 Co 9:6-7).

Joy has consistently given a good attitude and a lot
of love, regardless of the circumstances. I have learned
that I have the freedom to choose how I will respond in
attitude and action to any given situation. If I want
friends, I have to be a friend and not let little things
bother me.

When I feel unloved, then I start giving love, regardless of how I feel. Joy is needy with God and needy
before other people, but she expects that need to be
filled by God and not other people. God created the op-
posite of the 'vicious cycle'. He created His cycle of Life
to take its place. *If you [really] love Me, you will keep
(obey) My commands* (Jo 14:15). *If you keep My commandments [if you continue to obey My instructions],
you will abide in My love and live on in it, just as I
have obeyed My Father's commandments and live on in
His love* (Jo 15:10). So if I love Him, I'll obey and if I
obey, I'll love Him.

I am learning to be obedient, even in my lack, because when I am weak He is my Strength. He will always provide for me. "My husband Hershel was a great
encourager. 'Honey,' he would say, 'You can do it. You
can do anything you want to.' And to prove it, he gave
me everything to do. I did everything he told me to do.
I did everything but take over the pastorate!"

9. Enjoy the Ride

*In accord with the evangel of the glory of the happy
God . . . the happy and only Potentate will be showing:
He is King of Kings and Lord of Lords"* (1 Ti 1:11; 6:15
CLNT). This is the Concordant Literal New Testament
translation. I like holding on to a happy God!

Joy doesn't seem to hold on to anything too tightly,

only Jesus. She is not easily offended and readily laughs at herself. Like Joy, I am learning not to take myself too seriously. I only take God seriously at His Word.

When Zach lost his health at the pinnacle of his life, the only thing he had left was the Bible. He felt it was the only thing he could turn to. God's Word became a living, breathing reality to Zach.

One night when he was deep in fervent prayer, Zach sought God. He heard a soft voice telling him not to doubt God's words. After that night, his symptoms worsened before his heart was healed. But Zach took God seriously and held on to His words in his darkest moments.

Because he learned to hold on to Jesus at His Word, he doesn't take his circumstances as seriously as he used to. He enjoys the ride more because he enjoys Jesus and abides in Him.

Joy's son Tommy used to say in every Mother's Day sermon, "I am half man, half woman. My father was a man, and my mother was a woman!" We embrace both our feminine and masculine sides because we believe God has both masculine and feminine sides. We embrace who we are but don't take ourselves too seriously.

Since God speaks through all our circumstances, as long as I see Him in this principle, there will be meaning in all that happens. She showed me how to just be happy.

One morning, as I raced to school so the kids wouldn't be late, I was exasperated by my own stress and was putting it on the kids. I finally looked at them in the rearview mirror, sighed with acceptance, and said, "Oh, well, if we're late, we're late. Let's just enjoy the ride!"

It became a real-life metaphor whenever we would feel rushed. I don't know what lies ahead, so I just enjoy the ride, each and every day. This is what I want to pass on to my children. As I live my life each day, waking up and finding meaning in all the details, things both scheduled and unexpected, I live each day with purpose.

God trains those whom He calls. And it's definitely worth the work. It takes time and patience, so enjoy the ride.

Joy passed to me her prayer about this: "I'm not worried when people tell me that I committed some sin, or when the doctor said I have to die, and I was a young 34-year-old mother. I love You, and I trust You. I commit my life, if it's a moment, a day, a week, or a year, my life is Yours." She went on to explain, "And that's when God healed me. Faith is not a struggle. It is a rest. It was right there in front of me! It took a near fatal heart attack when I was only 34 to learn and accept this. Faith is not a struggle, it is a rest."

10. Give Unconditional Love

There is no fear in love [dread does not exist], but full-grown (complete, perfect) love turns fear out of doors and expels every trace of terror! For fear brings with it the thought of punishment, and [so] he who is afraid has not reached the full maturity of love [is not yet grown into love's complete perfection] (1 Jo 4:18).

This scripture is the summation of Joy's mentoring me. She taught me how to love. Her love matured me, brought down my walls of distrust, made it safe for me to grow up, and most importantly, to pass on this life to my husband, my children, my loved ones, and all those whose paths I cross.

Joy lived a life of love and passed it on to her family. Now I do the same for my four beautiful children. I've made more mistakes than I ever thought I would or wanted to, but I love my children no matter what.

Joy's love in action won her children to Jesus. There's nothing I can say to evangelize my children. I simply love them.

In Saint Theresa of Avila's book, *The Way of Perfection*, she believed that someone who truly loves in spirit doesn't really care whether they receive the affection of another or not. Love's essence is to love others for their spiritual profit, not for our own comfort or benefit. When we love in this way, we are happier to give than to receive, even in our relationship with the Creator Himself. What Saint Theresa described is holy affection. It is the only thing deserving its high and holy name: "love." As Joy said to me so many years ago, "Honey, I will love you, no matter what."

Personal Process Assessment

More is caught than taught. Catching what you see is an integral part of the learning process. What do you see in your friend that you want to catch? What do you see in your friend that you have and want to pass on?

Process is everything. By definition, process is a continuing development involving many changes; it is a particular method of doing a number of steps or operations.

You have to be willing, and you have to catch the lessons you see in your mentor if you want to learn. As a mentor, you need to be patient with the process. If you keep on doing the same old thing, you'll keep on getting what you've always gotten.

Are you willing to do differently? Are you willing to risk a new outcome by employing new actions and behavior?

My personality makes me unique, but I don't think I am different from anyone else in regard to my human nature. Joy and I are sharing our experience, strength, and hope with you, but some of these lessons will mean more to you than others because our personalities and experiences are all different. You must learn your own lessons from your own issues of life.

I had to learn how to forgive at a deeper level than most. That's where Joy's uniqueness and mine joined so that I could catch what I needed. Mentoring teaches the basics and also tailor teaches those lessons needed.

Our uniqueness has common ground which is why Joy and I fit so well. And why I learned those lessons tailor-made for me from her. Do you have the basics down? Do you see the tailor-made lessons you need to learn or share?

Top 10 Lessons I "Caught" From Joy

1. Be Myself
2. Live an Attitude of Forgiveness
3. Emotions Give Strength to My Decisions
4. When I Abide in Christ, He Answers My Prayers
5. Listen with My Heart
6. Keep a "Yes! Now!" Attitude
7. God Leads Me Down Unchosen Paths
8. Give What I Don't Have
9. Enjoy the Ride
10. Give Unconditional Love

Willingness is the contingency clause to the learning process. Are you willing to make yourself available to those relationships that are most meaningful to you?

God sees our lives like a movie, the scenes changing, the plots thickening, the climax building, and the happy ending. We believe God has a happy ending for your movie, and mentoring helps you get there. Hold on to the lessons you catch!

Why <u>not</u> go out on a limb? That's where the fruit is.

Mark Twain

Elijah and Elisha were going from Gilgal . . . And Elijah said to Elisha, Tarry here, I pray you, for the Lord has sent me to Bethel. But Elisha replied, As the Lord lives and as your soul lives, I will not leave you . . .the two of them went over on dry ground. And when they had gone over, Elijah said to Elisha, Ask what I shall do for you before I am taken from you. And Elisha said, I pray you, let a double portion of your spirit be upon me. He said, You have asked a hard thing. However, if you see me when I am taken from you, it shall be so for you—but if not, it shall not be so . . . and Elijah went up by a whirlwind into heaven. And Elisha saw it and . . . he took up also the mantle of Elijah that fell from him and went back and stood by the bank of the Jordan.

2 Kings 2:1-13

CHAPTER SEVEN
Leave a Lasting Legacy

And Elijah went up by a whirlwind into heaven. And Elisha saw it. When the sons of the prophets who were [watching] at Jericho saw him, they said, The spirit of Elijah rests on Elisha.

2 Kings 2:11-12,15

It's not how much we give. It's how much love goes with it.

Mother Teresa of Calcutta (1910-1997)

All endeavor calls for the ability to tramp the last mile, shape the last plan, endure the last hours toil. The fight to the finish spirit is the one . . . characteristic we must possess if we are to face the future as finishers.

Henry David Thoreau

And let the peace (soul harmony which comes) from Christ rule (act as umpire continually) in your hearts [deciding and settling with finality all questions that arise in your minds, in that peaceful state] to which as [members of Christ's] one body you were also called [to live]. And be thankful (appreciative), [giving praise to God always].

Colossians 3:15

Joy's past became my present. Her hindsight became my insight. I needed Joy's legacy. Without it I could not have become who I am. This is mentoring's purpose. Without God's life flowing in and through her, I could not have become who God meant me to be or daily fulfill His purposes as effectively as I do now. Her wisdom equipped me for the calling. *Wisdom is justified and vindicated by what she does (her deeds) and by her children* (Ma 11:19). She didn't pass the baton until I was strong enough to carry it. It took time to reach that point, but that's part of the process.

Joy inculcated her life into mine so I could live those principles learned with those around me. To inculcate is to teach and impress by frequent repetitions or admonitions. Its synonym is implant. My soul was fertile soil for her to plant God's seeds of life that would take root and grow and blossom. *Let the word [spoken by] Christ (the Messiah) have its home [in your hearts and minds] and dwell in you in [all its] richness, as you teach and admonish and train one another in all insight and intelligence and wisdom [in spiritual things, and as you sing] psalms and hymns and spiritual songs, making melody to God with [His] grace in your hearts* (Col 3:16).

When Michael asked if I was interested in co-hosting a radio show he created in Washington, D.C., I consented, confident in faith, but not yet seeing the calling.

So many of God's principles that flowed through Joy were being deployed. God's purposes were being fulfilled. It was a path that I did not intend to take, nor ever expected to. I kept a "yes, now" attitude, enjoyed a great ride, listened with my heart, and learned to love everyone.

Once the taping started, there was no editing or stopping, so I had to keep going, even when I stumbled. In the frustration of my imperfection, my husband smiled and quietly encouraged me, "Don't be afraid to fail." Those words became the premise to my approach.

The wisdom learned in my recovery resonated in my mind, "I came to Al-Anon perfect, and only got worse." Actually, my shortcomings endeared our listeners with a greater sense of connectedness.

The big payoff was a wonderful and real recovery talk show that moved smoothly, touched hearts deeply, and brought closure to tough topics with healing and understanding. Joy's past became a present to me and all those who listened as well. The intrinsic and most important payoff was what was going on inside— learning to be authentic. I would rather die trying and failing than never try at all.

Joy's mentoring saved me from the realm of the unconscious. Unconscious motives can be pretty powerful until they are brought out into the light. Once exposed, they begin losing their potency. My selfish ways served me well, until they were exposed by Joy's wisdom and actions.

I was taking piano lessons when my daughters were young, and Joy offhandedly mentioned how she stopped playing so she could focus on Tommy's piano lessons. She doesn't know this, but I knew God was speaking through her past to become my present. I stopped playing and focused on each of my four children's music lessons. It was their turn.

Some of Jesus' last words were, *Father forgive them, for they know not what they do* (Lk 23:34). He was speaking of our unconscious, those sinful areas in our lives yet to be exposed and understood by us.

Mentoring brought me into the conscious through what I call Spiritual Situational Awareness. Situational awareness is an integral part of piloting aircraft and boats. It's knowing what's going on around you. Pilots have to be able to identify, process, and understand critical elements of information in order to safely and effectively navigate. This awareness protects them from turbulence and storms, saves lives, and enables them to reach their intended destination.

Spiritual Situational Awareness is becoming cognizant of what's going on inside you. It's recognizing the issues of your life. Joy's mentoring has helped me to safely and effectively navigate my life. Her hindsight was often the forecast that saved me from a lot of turbulent life storms!

I learned to see God in the clouds and through the clouds. The sun doesn't stop shining just because there are clouds. It is still there doing its work. Yes, clouds produce rain, but instead of being washed away by the storm, I let God's healing *reign* wash over me.

It's not just reading God's Word daily that is important to me but how I read it. When I open the Bible to my planned reading for each day, I expect to hear from God and really believe with all my heart each and every word is Holy Spirit inspired and God ordained. I also believe I am reading what I am meant to read in that moment in time.

When I pray it is usually with the discipline of letting go of daily mundane and routine thoughts that clutter my mind. Although I prefer to have quiet time in the early morning and at bedtime, sometimes my quiet time comes in little increments throughout the day. I don't think God really cares when I have my quiet time. He just wants me to love Him and care about Him. And if I lose my serenity and sanity over something, I can start a new 24 hours anytime.

Hilary's rape put her in the position of having to face herself at her deepest level spiritually. She chose to face what happened and let her aunt Jen mentor her and help her through it. Jen helped Hilary become spiritually aware of what took place.

First, Hilary was cognizant even in the middle of the rape that Jesus was with her. Second, she chose in this defining moment to forgive the rapist and speak out against this atrocity to help others. Third, as soon as she felt strong enough emotionally, Hilary started speaking in high schools and other public places about rape awareness.

There are three essential parts of Spiritual Situational Awareness:

1. Awareness: Knowing what is going on inside of you. Defining moments reveal your purpose and bring you to that place of understanding.
2. Appraisal: Once you understand, ignorance is no longer an option. You have to choose how you will respond. The power of choice is a God-given gift.
3. Action: Doing is the cement that holds your purpose intact. I do and I become.

Spiritual Situational Awareness is a vital daily discipline for me that keeps me abiding in Jesus:

1. Awareness: I paint a mental picture of being a leaf on the Vine. I ask myself, am I staying grafted or am I trying to do things my way? *I am the Vine; you are the branches. Whoever lives in Me and I in him bears much (abundant) fruit. However, apart from Me [cut off from vital union with Me] you can do nothing* (Jo 15:5).
2. Appraisal: Am I staying conscious of my attitude, abiding in Jesus, and bringing my thoughts and purposes captive to the obedience of my Lord Jesus? *We lead every thought and purpose away captive into the obedience of Christ (the Messiah, the Anointed One)* (2 Co 10:5).

3. Action: The music I listen to, the friends I keep, the movies I watch, and the words I say will line up with His Word and His Will. *You are My friends if you keep on doing the things which I command you to do* (Jo 15:14).

Joy left a lasting legacy when her past became the present for so many of her counseled recipients. Steve came to Joy angry and brokenhearted after losing his job. He needed Spiritual Situational Awareness.

He was highly trained for the job he had recently acquired and took great pride in doing it with excellence. He was told that promotions were based on hard work and qualifications.

Pouring his heart into his work, giving one hundred and ten percent to months of consistent effort, the time came for promotion to be announced. He knew he had done all he could to prove himself worthy of the promotion. His coworkers also believed he would receive it. But a recently hired man having no previous experience (who was a friend of someone in upper management) received the promotion.

Steve was devastated. After expressing his perplexity and dissatisfaction to his manager, he was taken to the division manager who told him one of the main reasons he was passed over was because when given a task to do, he did that task and more, trying to improve things they didn't want improved.

After talking for an hour in that office and getting nowhere, they proceeded to the general manager's office. The general manager expressed the same reasoning adding, "You have a good personality for leadership, but you need to work on your shortcomings.

"We cannot help you. You need leadership training, but in the meantime you cannot work here." So after almost two hours of fruitless discussions with three managers, Steve was escorted off the property as though he were a criminal. He was more baffled than ever before.

One thing that kept going through his mind as he drove home was the scrutinizing scowl in the general manager's eyes. He had noticed this look, but could never figure out what made him feel so uncomfortable around him until now. In that look he could see his stepfather glaring at him, sending the same message. It was a look of disapproval and disgust as though he just couldn't stand Steve's presence. He didn't get along with his stepfather until years after leaving home and receiving Jesus into his life. By now Steve felt confused, frustrated, and uncertain of his future. In his own words, he felt "lower than a snake's belly." It was a defining moment, but he didn't know what to do.

Hearing about Joy, he chanced calling her. As they sat, the words started out slow but gradually gained momentum as he recounted what happened. Steve sat before this petite woman, her sage confidence shrouded in peace, his huge frame racked with heavy sobbing.

They joined hands and prayed a simple prayer for God to give them wisdom. As their conversation unfolded, the Holy Spirit was there, walking through each step with them and giving clear new insight as the past was laid before them.

As Joy's mentoring wisdom took hold in Steve's heart, he could see clearly. The feelings he had experienced with his stepfather resurfaced, and he felt he could never do anything right. Their encounters always ended in rejection, and the same was happening in this new job where he so wanted to win approval and acceptance.

This defining moment cried out, demanding a response. Steve's mind, now totally clear and open before

God, instantly grasped the truth. This insecure, condemned man was not the real person. "*You* are the real person, designed by God," Joy encouraged him, "A person of great value."

As the clouds of condemnation that had cloaked his spark of divinity were blown away by God's revelation, Steve could see clearly who he really was. The sense of greatness that is in everyone was uncovered.

The spark of divinity, eternally placed in each of us by God, was ignited. Now that his spirit, soul, and body were working in perfect symphonic relationship, his greatest dreams could be accomplished.

In that defining moment, Steve chose to accept himself as God sees him and not someone else's constricted, condemning view. He began speaking with a new, unthreatened confidence.

Now that Steve was aware of what was going on inside his heart, he appraised the situation and made positive choices based on his fresh knowledge. He was ready to cement his Spiritual Situational Awareness by taking the third step—action.

He told family members about past feelings and problems he had experienced. He realized his reactions to his feelings, although unpleasant to those around him, were very normal considering the pain he had endured in his childhood. He spoke of the relief he felt when he learned that many problems with deep roots could be dealt with. Knowing the reasons why he felt that way allowed him to be freed.

Yet Steve had dreaded the talk with Joy, thinking he couldn't stand hearing one more time that he had a bad attitude. So many times he had heard criticism without help for change. He already knew he had a problem. He just didn't know how to fix it. But instead of criticism, Steve found in Joy acceptance from a compassionate, caring Christian who had the knowledge and insight to understand him and the wisdom to help him. Her past became Steve's present.

Within months, the owner of a business that Steve had done some side work for asked if he would be interested in a part-time job. Steve accepted, and two weeks after going to work the owner offered him a full-time position as manager, telling him he had the ability, knowledge, and skills to run a business.

He is still there, running the business with purpose and without those self-condemning tapes that used to run through his mind. Steve let his Spiritual Situational Awareness work for him.

Leaving a lasting legacy comes only through people, not things. One of the most significant leaders in our country's history left a lasting legacy because his defining moments revealed his purpose:

1831- Failed in business
1832- Defeated for legislature
1833- Second failure in business
1836- Suffers nervous breakdown
1838- Defeated for Speaker
1840- Defeated for Elector
1843- Defeated for Congress
1848- Defeated for Congress
1855- Defeated for Senate
1856- Defeated for Vice President
1858- Defeated for Senate
1860- Elected President

This was Abraham Lincoln's road to the White House. Almost 30 years later, after his first business failure and the many other failures that followed, he became president of our country during the bloodiest war in American history.

His "failures" were probably the scaffolding that

built the fortitude and character necessary to run our nation during such a vulnerable and tumultuous time. So often what we see as stumbling blocks, God sees as building blocks for the structure we need inside to handle His will and blessings.

We have a family motto: "Take the blame. Get the blessing." If I am not willing to admit when I am wrong and choose to practice militant ignorance instead, the same lesson is going to keep popping up for me to deal with until I am willing to cross that bridge.

Adam started the blame game, and we still play it well. "God, it's the woman you gave me" is a difficult attitude to escape. Pointing the finger at the other person is far easier than accepting responsibility.

It's okay to be wrong, to make mistakes, to fail. It doesn't mean that I am a mistake or a failure. We have to separate the action from the person. It is far more important to be happy than to be "right," I learned in recovery. You don't have to have a mentor to understand the defining moments in your life, but mentoring provides counsel and wisdom that enable you to see your purpose, broadens your choices, and strengthens your character to be all who you are meant to become. It is a two-way relationship that creates a roadway where the older and wiser passes life lessons on to the younger and ignorant. We're talking about a worthwhile friendship that is meant to last a lifetime and leave a legacy of eternal value. Both parties benefit.

Your destiny is what is meant to be. Your purpose is the intent or determination of your heart. Meaning is the message. It is the significance of or reason behind your goal. Your goal is the target or task set before you. It is dependent upon your destiny, purpose, and meaning.

Joy's destiny is heaven; her purpose is to help people who hurt. Her meaning for living is Jesus, and her goal is to counsel those in need of her gift of encouragement. My destiny is heaven; my purpose is to use my gift of encouragement. My meaning for living is to have fellowship with God in Jesus, and my goal is to use my gift in any capacity. I wake up with purpose every day and see significance in everything that happens and what God places before me.

In my capacity as wife and mom, I am loving, encouraging, supporting, and speaking life into the situation. I am not perfect. I can just as easily cross over into an unsightly space if I don't take care of myself.

In 12-step recovery, I learned to HALT when I am Hungry, Angry, Lonely, or Tired. Staying disciplined to take care of myself is a conscious commitment. I love my life. Joy loves her life. This is such an incredible gift just to say that!

God showed me how to FRET not. So at the cross I leave Fear, Resentment, Envy, and Toxic anger. *Cease from anger and forsake wrath; fret not yourself—it tends only to evildoing* (Ps 37:8).

You have to want it. The secret is desire. When you identify your desire, you will find your purpose. The desire is your call. Misplaced desire is misspent desire. Your spirit is like a vacuum that was meant to be filled with God and by God. And the contingency clause is willingness. You just need to show up and be willing.

We were meant to be well—spirit, soul, and body. Because we are a threefold being, when one of these areas is damaged, it will affect the others. Healing begets healing. The results of spiritual and emotional healing often bring emotional and physical healing in their wake.

You are second to none. You are unique, unlike any other. You are meant to make a difference. You are born with the spark of divinity. It is the spark that ignites the fire. God birthed in you this feeling of greatness, which becomes the foundation upon which your dream is built. It is not of you, and that is why it stays in your heart.

The events that take place in our life define us and impel us. These defining moments birth in you a desire that determines or directs your destiny. It may have been a recurring event or a one-time experience. Regardless, it defines you and reveals your purpose.

Emotions give strength to our decisions when they instruct us, speaking to the bigger picture. They validate decisions resulting from your defining moments. God uses these defining moments to bring forth the gifts given you and already in you.

Mentoring brings you to your zenith and keeps you there. When Edith walked into Maria's office, little did they know how far their relationship would take them. But they both perceived in their spirits a sense of well-being with each other, kind of like they were meant to meet. They both acted on this. When Maria needed an assistant to accompany her on one of her mission trips, Edith filled the position. When Edith needed someone to help her deal with what was going on around her and inside of her, Maria was a safe person to vent with.

Maria's wisdom, integrity, and willingness to share her life with Edith helped catapult Edith into a God-ordained position of fulfilling His purposes in her life. During the 11 years, their trusted friendship developed into such a meaningful relationship that Maria mentored Edith and brought about a depth of maturity where Maria felt safe enough to pass her ministry on to Edith. Edith runs the ministry with the same spirit passed on to her through Maria, all for the glory of God.

As I am in this moment of time, so shall I be when I get to heaven. That thought makes me want to be my best at all times. This doesn't mean that I am perfect or have to act perfect.

God left a lasting legacy through the relationship between Elijah and Elisha. In 1 Kings 19:12-21, He spoke to Elijah in a still voice in the wilderness and told Elijah to anoint Elisha. Elijah crossed over to Elisha and cast his mantle upon him. Elisha got up and followed Elijah.

Elijah trained Elisha for years, and when Elijah ascended, his mantle fell. Elisha took it and continued the same task God had put before Elijah, which was to destroy Baal worship in Israel.

Elijah's past became Elisha's present as Elisha acted upon what he learned from Elijah. Then, before he died, Elisha passed God's calling on to Jehu. This story is an outstanding example of mentoring in its finest form. This relationship is all about God.

God's purpose was in all they did, said, thought, and prayed. Can you imagine seeing a chariot of fire engulfed in flames coming down from heaven and taking away your best friend? What an awesome defining moment that must have been for Elisha!

Elisha's defining moment revealed his purpose. Elisha wanted to follow in Elijah's footsteps. He chose to give glory to God, look to God, and be obedient to the calling. Elijah left a trail like none other, and Elisha wanted to follow God. Elisha followed God through Elijah.

Joy and I are not Elijah and Elisha, but the dynamics are the same. We clearly see how our friendship was meant to be, that it is about God and not us, so we give God the glory for everything. Although God is no respecter of people, He knew Joy would be best as my mentor. I would not be the person God meant me to be if it had not been for her influence in my life and my obedience to what God was saying through her.

When I prayed about this, asking God what I would do without Joy, I felt an immediate, almost imperceptible response in my spirit, quiet and clear, "When it is Joy's time to go, you won't need her anymore." God is my Provider, and I will have the wisdom He wants me to have to continue the calling He has for me. It's not about me; it's about God.

I turn to God through Joy. God uses her in my life to speak truth and cultivate wisdom more than most anyone in my life. She was His willing instrument.

I don't believe life is meant to be lived like a roller coaster. As I mature, the highs don't seem so high anymore; nor do the lows seem so low.

Perhaps I am learning to live more comfortably in a spiritual place of well-being. It feels so good to live inside my own skin and be at peace. By abiding in Jesus, I am happy. There is absolutely nothing under heaven or on earth that feels better than abiding in Jesus. His yoke may be easy and His burden light, but there is always death at the cross. *Take My yoke upon you and learn of Me, for I am gentle (meek) and humble (lowly) in heart, and you will find rest (relief and ease and refreshment and recreation and blessed quiet) for your souls. For My yoke is wholesome (useful, good—not harsh, hard, sharp, or pressing, but comfortable, gracious, and pleasant), and My burden is light and easy to be borne* (Ma 11:29-30). But when I leave my sin and myself at the cross, the seed of selfishness dies, and what springs forth in its place is a life of unspeakable peace that can only be understood by experience. The life that springs forth is the Life of Jesus.

What you feed grows. If I feed the flesh, then my selfishness grows. If I feed the spirit, my spirit grows. *And he who does not take up his cross and follow Me [cleave steadfastly to Me, conforming wholly to My example in living and, if need be, in dying also] is not worthy of Me. Whoever finds his [lower] life will lose it [the higher life], and whoever loses his [lower] life on My account will find it [the higher life]* (Ma 10:38-39).

Faith is a rest, not a struggle! *Come to Me, all you who labor and are heavy-laden and overburdened, and I will cause you to rest* (Ma 11:28). All I need to do is abide in Jesus. *I am the Vine; you are the branches. Whoever lives in Me and I in him bears much (abundant) fruit. However, apart from Me [cut off from vital union with Me] you can do nothing* (Jo 15:5). My self is not dead. I am dead to my self! My self is still strong and living, but it no longer has power over me. I must daily take up my cross and follow Jesus. You see, the baton Joy passed on to me is the cross of Jesus.

A mentoring friendship is a win-win relationship. The benefactor and beneficiary mutually benefit. Life is made more meaningful for both. When Joy passes the baton to me, she sees that I am the better for it, with the fruits of her life alive and working in me, making her life even more worthwhile.

This happens for Joy every time she passes the baton or blessing to someone else who catches it. Living life principles that work is better than beating my head against the wall. The connectedness we share is the best part of all.

What Aunt Jen passed on to Hilary was the cross of Jesus. God knew Jen was the best fit for Hilary. Hilary wrote the following note to her Aunt Jen on Jen's fiftieth birthday:

"When I think of Aunt Jen, I think of a person who loves the Lord and loves her family. She is the organizer of many a family get-together and is usually the one orchestrating the whole fiasco or event. Whether it is playing hand-and-foot or writing Thanksgiving poetry, Jen is always coming up with creative ways to improve our family togetherness.

"I am so thankful for the close-knit family we have and grateful for Jen's efforts to keep it that way. Although I've known Jen for my entire life, I have become infinitely closer to her in the past seven months. Jen has been a shoulder to cry on, a personal mentor, a spiritual leader, and a book-writing partner for me.

"She helped me get through the most difficult time of my life and motivated me to turn it into something positive. Jen's encouragement and amazing ideas have opened so many doors and created incredible opportunities for me. I cannot express my gratitude for her help, and I am excited for what lies ahead as she hopefully continues to work with me and be my 'manager.'

"So after many meetings at Einstein's Brother's Bagels, Starbucks, and Jen's home, I have developed a new appreciation for the wonderful woman who is my aunt. I am so blessed that God put Jen in my life, and I look forward to getting to know her even better in the future.

I am honored to have Aunt Jen as my aunt and even more honored to call her my friend."

Process is everything. All that we've shared with you is about processes that work when you work them. And it's worth it. Be willing. Be tenacious. Stay connected. Be at peace.

Let mentoring catapult you to your place of purpose and live it out. Nurture those divine relationships in your life that bring a wealth of love, insight, and understanding. Call on such friends whenever you feel like you're getting off track, and even when you're on target. It will validate your sense of divine appointment. It will validate their sense of divine purpose.

Joy left me a lasting legacy in encouragement. A God-given gift I was destined for, she brought it out in me and I chose to act on it. However, I had to change my thought patterns.

By instilling new habits and making healthy choices, encouragement reigns in my mind over doubt and discouragement regardless of circumstances. It has taken precedence over a lot of negative thinking.

Although I knew I had the gift of encouragement, it took years for me to become mature enough to handle the responsibility of the gift. I allowed Joy into the inner recesses of my needy soul, and she never took advantage of my vulnerability. Instead, she infused me with her own experience, strength, and integrity. She needed to be needed, and I needed her.

You find your purpose when your talent intersects your ability. Mentoring builds the roadway to reaching your potential and that intersection. It is the roadway of relationship.

The intimacy and understanding in our relationship gives us permission to be ourselves and enjoy every minute of our time together. One thing I've always appreciated about Joy is her perception of God as a practical God.

God is real and palpable to Joy and me. Being able to communicate my thoughts and feelings and confess my sins or shortcomings to someone wiser has imparted to me that same approach.

She taught me to be firm about keeping self-pity out of my life and not worry so much about someone else's stuff. My own list is long enough, let alone trying to take another's inventory.

Self-acceptance is a priceless gift and an essential element in defining humility. Living authentically is wonderful and worth the work. Her legacy continues through me, my children, and countless others willing to receive her wisdom and counsel.

Traveling and technology has helped broaden our

horizons, but often at the cost of keeping close relationships at bay. Often we're not close to parents, siblings, and loved ones who have helped define our lives. Mentoring has the potential and the power to stabilize our culture through its cohesive nature, to connect the past with the present and to catapult it into the future.

Before Dr. Bill Bright passed away, he felt God was telling him that the preservation of the church in the United States was dependent upon the preservation of pastors in our country. When Don lost his wife, his ministry, and his son, only one pastor and very few friends visited him. Was it because they didn't know what to do? Were they not equipped to deal with this depth of disaster?

A man can't give what he doesn't have, and we need to give pastors permission to be human. Perhaps we need to show our pastor more love, respect, and forgiveness and fill them up in such a way that they have it to give back when necessary. Don chose to step down and preserve the integrity of the office of pastor, and that may be one of the reasons his life is so full today without a deep sense of shame or a wake of spiritual carnage.

Andrew believes he'll backslide if he's not witnessing in his 12-step program and passing his life on to others. He believes this is vital to his recovery. He has seen men go right back into drinking when they just receive and don't reciprocate. At that point, even receiving will cease.

When the sower scattered the seed, only one of four took root. I remember this story so I don't get discouraged when I see a relationship in my life where my love and efforts are not reciprocated. I am not God, nor do I understand another's heart and mind. You won't always see when you make a difference. Sometimes it takes years before the harvest is ready.

God's timing is everything. Mary and Elizabeth were meant to meet.

And at that time Mary arose and went with haste into the hill country to a town of Judah. And she went to the house of Zachariah and, entering it, saluted Elizabeth. And it occurred that when Elizabeth heard Mary's greeting, the baby leaped in her womb, and Elizabeth was filled with and controlled by the Holy Spirit. And she cried out with a loud cry, and then exclaimed, Blessed (favored of God) above all other women are you! And blessed (favored of God) is the Fruit of your womb! And how [have I deserved that this honor should] be granted to me, that the mother of my Lord should come to me? For behold, the instant the sound of your salutation reached my ears, the baby in my womb leaped for joy.

Luke 1:39-44

Mary and Elizabeth complemented each other, understood each other and shared what is probably the most fascinating and phenomenal mentoring friendship in the history of mankind. Even their babies fit! They clearly saw the significance of God in their friendship. Both loved the Lord, were married, pregnant for the first time, and knew they were going to have sons. And not just any sons, but Mary would give birth to the Son of God while Elizabeth would give birth to the prophet paving the way for the Son of God. An extremely rare knowledge of gender, given no ultrasound at the time! For both had visitations from God, and in both cases, their defining moments took the form of the angel Gabriel (see Lk 1:19,26). Yet they were different, with different backgrounds, and Elizabeth was older and long married. They found and filled the need in each other for deep and meaningful understanding, spiritual fulfillment, and just comfortable camaraderie.

Sharing such similar experiences, Mary and Elizabeth had simpatico together, knowing how each other felt physically, emotionally, and spiritually. Elizabeth was older and farther along in her pregnancy, and she was able to share life experiences and feelings that probably helped make the load lighter for such a lonely, young, vulnerable girl. Together they shared meals, chores, dreams, expectations and all those little things about pregnancy that when shared, make the burden of pregnancy bearable. *And Mary remained with her [Elizabeth] for about three months and [then] returned to her [own] home* (Lk 1:56). In an age where women were treated like second-class citizens and her husband had grounds for divorce having a wife pregnant not by him, Elizabeth's mentoring helped Mary hold on to her life's purpose in a way no one else could. They were together in this moment in time determining the destiny of mankind forever.

Silenced by Gabriel for his doubt, Elizabeth's husband Zachariah must have had tremendous respect for Mary's faith. *And there appeared to him an angel of the Lord . . . and when Zachariah saw him, he was troubled, and fear took possession of him* (Lk 1:11-12). Mary's response, however, differed radically. *The angel Gabriel was sent from God to a town of Galilee named Nazareth, To a girl never having been married and a virgin engaged to be married to a man whose name was Joseph, a descendant of the house of David; and the virgin's name was Mary. . . . But when she saw him, she was greatly troubled and disturbed and confused at what he said and kept revolving in her mind what such a greeting might mean . . . Then Mary said, Be-*

*hold, I am the handmaiden of the Lord; let it be done to
me according to what you have said* (Lk 1:26,27,29,38).

May each one of us learn to let Mary's response be
our response as we let the Holy Spirit as our Holy
Mentor give us understanding into the deep truth of
this mentoring wisdom! When God speaks, don't let
fear preside and possess you; rather let it pass and let
those thoughts revolve in your mind and understand
what His greeting means to you. God speaks through
the circumstances of life. Let His natural laws lead
you to His spiritual principles as Mary and Elizabeth
did.

The fruits of mentoring are the richest rewards but
are produced when ripe and ready. Be patient with the
process. Being whole is being who you are meant to be,
living in trust and living with a strong spiritual sense
of well-being.

Remember, your desire is your call. It is a want-to,
not a have-to. Love motivates. Mentoring will fast-
forward you rapidly.

Mentoring is founded in friendship, where the past
becomes the present. It is more than just about learning to do it right. It is about connectedness and relationship.

The life flows through the relationship. The connectedness is what makes it safe to fail, get up, hold
on, and continue. When I piously encouraged my dad,
"God is a second-chance God," he gave me the best reply ever. "God is not a second-chance God," he exclaimed. "He is another-chance God!" Sometimes I
have to keep falling and getting up before I get it
right.

Let Him change your spirit! Only He can do it. You
only have to want it. There is a backup plan waiting
just for you. Your life has great purpose and destiny.

Holding on to meaningful life principles and leaving a lasting legacy take time, but it's worth the work. God alone is worthy and God knows you're worth it!

Personal Process Assessment

Joy's hindsight became my insight. God knew I needed Joy's example to follow so that I might fulfill His purposes for my life. Without her loving, trusted friendship, I could not have become who I am. This is mentoring's purpose. When I acted on her wisdom, it became a part of me. I didn't just listen. I listened, processed, and acted upon her wisdom so it became a part of me and what she leaves behind. A lasting legacy has eternal value. Anyone can leave just money or objects. *The things that are visible are temporal (brief and fleeting), but the things that are invisible are deathless and everlasting* (2 Co 4:18). What is your legacy? Is it lasting?

If you keep on doing what you've always done, you'll keep on getting what you've always gotten. How will you make different choices that keep you on track and focused?

Your life has great purpose now, not later. *Behold, now is the day of salvation* (2 Co 6:2). For being such a little word, "now" packs a lot of punch. Are you acting on what you are learning? Are you taking time to pass on your life to someone you know needs you? Valued friendships are just that. They are valued because they are expensive. You get what you pay for. Are you investing in your valued relationships? If so, how?

In my recovery program, I learned the major issue in my life was control, how fearful I really was, and how to let go and let God. I used to try so hard and push for my way. I learned an ounce of example is worth a pound of advice, and it is a program of attraction rather than promotion. Drawn by God calling precedes driven by purpose. How are you making yourself attractive? Are you hearing God calling you? Are you taking time to listen? And love Him?

The baton was passed, but I had to be strong enough to carry it. It took time to reach that point. Elijah's past became Elisha's present, and it was all about God's calling on them. It was all about God. It is still all about God! Who is your Elisha? Are you willing to pass the mantle? Who is your Elijah? Do you see your mantle? Are you willing to take it?

Mentoring helps us safely navigate our life and stay the course through Spiritual Situational Awareness. These three simple steps are:

1. Awareness: Knowing what's going on inside your heart.
2. Appraisal: Choice based on understanding.
3. Action: Doing means becoming who God meant you to be.

The baton Joy passed to me is the cross of Jesus. His yoke may be easy and His burden light, but there is always death at the cross. The seed of self-centeredness dies, and the Life of Jesus takes its place. That is why I can feel so good and at peace with myself, even when I stumble. Who encourages you to be closer to Jesus? What are they passing on to you? What are you passing on to them? Are you pushing each other closer to Jesus?

Make your life worth following. Remember we want you to hold on to the truth that mentoring helps you find out what you want and live with purpose. It encourages you to hold on to what you want until you get it. Hold on!

———•·•◦•———

Our highest goal is to become like our Lord Christ in the beauty of many virtues—that is, in humility, purity and zeal to do only the will of God. It is this goal—to imitate the spirit of our Lord—that we must maintain.

Bernard of Clairvaux (1090-1153)

Never think that God's delays are God's denials.
Hold on, hold fast, hold out. Patience is genius.

Comte Georges Louis Leclerc de Buffon

Wisdom is justified and vindicated by what she does (her deeds) and by her children.

Matthew 11:19

"Where there is no vision [no redemptive revelation of God], the people perish" (Pr 29:18), but where there are no people, the vision will perish.

Joy Barnett,
on the Dream Center in Los Angeles

I am coming soon. Hold on to what you have, so that no one will take your crown.

Revelation 3:11 (NIV)

For more information on mentoring, go to:
www.makeadifferencementoring.com